THE ULTIMATE TOWER AIR FRYER COOKBOOK

1001-Day Frugal, Tasty and Low-calorie Recipes for Popular Restaurant Meals You Can Make at Home

Copyright©2023 Georgia Harris
All rights reserved. No part of this book may be reproduced or used in any manner without the prior written permission of the copyright owner, except for the use of brief quotations in a book review.
First paperback edition May 2023.
Cover art by Natalie M. Kern
Printed by Amazon in the USA.
Disclaimer : Although the author and publisher have made every effort to ensure that the information in this book was correct at press time, the author and publisher do not assume and hereby disclaim any liability to any party for any loss, damage, or disruption caused by errors or omissions, whether such errors or omissions result from negligence, accident, or any other cause. this book is not intended as a substitute for the medical advice of physicians.

CONTENTS

INTRODUCTION 6

BREAKFAST & BRUNCH RECIPES 8

    Air Fryer Breakfast Burritos 8
    Buttermilk Pancakes 8
    Leftover Turkey Pot Pie 8
    Air Fryer Tex Mex Egg Rolls 9
    Spice Empanadas 9
    Air-fryer Hash Brown 10
    Scallion Pancake 11
    Air Fryer French Onion Tarts 11
    Air Fryer Pierogies With Onions 12
    Air Fryer Poached Eggs 12
    Air Fryer Hard Boiled Eggs 13
    Reuben Egg Rolls 13
    Air Fryer Chunky Monkey French Toast ...13
    Five Cheese Pull Apart Bread 14
    Tinga Cauliflower Tacos 14
    Air Fryer Hand Pies 15
    Air Fryer French Toast Sticks 16
    Steamed Cinnamon Buns 16
    Air Fryer Egg Rolls 17
    Air Fryer Falafel 17
    Air Fryer Bacon Cinnamon Rolls 18
    Air Fryer Cinnamon Rolls 18
    Homemade Air Fryer Pizza Rolls 19
    Air Fryer Frozen Texas Toast 20
    Air Fryer Egg Bites 20

DESSERTS RECIPES 21

    Chocolate Chickpea Bites 21
    Salted Caramel Snickerdoodle Cookie 21
    Homemade Cannoli 21
    Air Fryer Halloween Ghost Cupcakes 22
    Air Fryer Berry Crisp 23
    Air Fryer Blueberry Hand Pies 23
    Air Fryer Cream Cheese Cherry Pies 24
    Air Fryer Strawberry Nutella Hand Pies 25
    Air Fryer Donuts 25
    Apple Pie In The Air Fryer 25
    Air Fryer Baked Apples 26
    Air Fryer Doubletree Signature Cookie 27
    Air Fryer Biscuits 27
    Air Fryer Ice Cream Cookie Sandwich 27
    Air-fryer Brownies 28
    Grammy's Jam Thumbprints 28
    Air Fryer Frozen Turnover Pastries 28
    Air Fryer Celebration Bites 29
    Air Fried Oreos 29
    Leek & Mushroom Pie 29
    Air Fryer Grilled Cheese 30
    Roast Dinner Yorkshire Pudding Wraps ...31
    How To Cook Patty Pan Squash 31
    Air Fryer Molten Lava Cakes 32

POULTRY RECIPES 33

    Italian Chicken Skewers 33
    Air Fryer Frozen Chicken Pot Pie 33
    Air Fryer Southern Fried Chicken 33
    Air Fryer Chicken Wings 33
    Air Fryer Bone In Chicken Thighs 34
    Air Fryer Yogurt Marinated Chicken 34

Air Fryer Turkey Meatloaf 35	Butter-herb Roasted Whole Chicken 39
Air Fryer Boneless Chicken Thighs 35	Jerk Chicken Wings 40
Air-fryer Buffalo Wings 36	Air Fryer Crispy Chicken Breasts 40
Bbq Chicken Wings 36	Chicken Shawarma Flatbreads 40
Air Fryer Chicken Strips 36	Air Fryer Orange Chicken From Frozen 41
Air Fryer Chicken Cordon Bleu 37	Air Fryer Chicken Stuffed 42
Kfc Nashville Hot Chicken Tenders 37	Chipotle, Honey & Lime Wings 42
Air Fryer Buffalo Chicken Egg Rolls 38	Air Fried Chicken 43
Crispy Air Fryer Chicken Thighs 38	5 Ingredient Crispy Cheesy 43
Air Fryer Chicken Kabobs 39	Air Fryer General Tso's Chicken 44

BEEF, PORK & LAMB RECIPES 45

Air Fryer Beef Jerky 45	Lamb Kofta & Aubergine Wedges 50
Beef Wellingtons And Potatoes 45	Air Fryer Meatloaf Recipe 51
Crispy Pork Belly 46	Air Fryer Corned Beef 52
Air Fryer Ham 46	Juicy Air Fryer Meatballs 52
Prunes In Bacon 47	Air Fryer Mexican Pizza 53
Roasted Cauliflower Steaks 47	Air Fryer Lemon And Herb Pork 53
Air Fryer Bacon Wrapped Avocado 48	Air Fryer Bacon 54
Spicy Air Fryer Pork Belly 48	Bacon Wrapped Brussel Sprouts 54
Brussels & Bacon Flatbread 49	How To Make Bacon In The Air Fryer 54
Air-fryer Beef Wellington Wontons 49	Air Fryer Full English 55
Air Fryer Meatballs 50	Frozen Pork Chops In The Air Fryer 55
Meat Platter With Pap, Chakalaka 50	

FISH & SEAFOOD RECIPES 56

Salmon Catnip Cat Treats 56	Air Fryer Salmon 60
Air Fryer Salmon With Skin 56	Air Fryer Fish 60
Air Fryer Shrimp 56	Air Fryer Salmon And Brussels Sprouts 61
Air Fryer Scallops 57	Frozen Salmon In The Air Fryer 61
Blackened Air Fryer Salmon Bites 57	Air Fryer Lemon Garlic Shrimp 62
Air Fryer Honey Sriracha Salmon 58	Harissa Salmon With Crispy Chickpeas 62
Air Fryer Mexican Shrimp 58	Airfried Teriyaki Salmon 62
Coconut Prawns 59	Crunchy Salmon Circle Cat Treats 63
Air Fryer Cajun Shrimp Dinner 59	Air Fried Popcorn Prawns 63
Air Fryer Frozen Shrimp 59	Air Fryer Fish Sticks 64

Bacon-wrapped Shrimp In Air Fryer 64
Air Fryer Bacon Wrapped Scallops 65
Air Fryer Shrimp Tacos 65
Air Fryer Coconut-fried Shrimp 66
Air-fryer Salmon Cakes 66
Lemon-garlic Air Fryer Salmon 66
Cajun Air Fryer Salmon 67
Striped Bass With Radish Salsa Verde 67

SALADS & SIDE DISHES RECIPES 68

Pita Chips & Hummus 68
Air Fryer Sauteed Onions 68
Air Fryer Falafel Salad 68
Tuna Egg Salad 69
Air Fryer Green Bean Casserole 69
Crispy Smashed Potatoes 69
Spicy Canned Salmon Salad Rice Bowl 70
Chicken Caprese Salad Recipe 70
Air Fryer Bacon Stuffed Jalapenos 71
Grilled Peach & Burrata Salad 71
Colcannon Croquettes 72

SANDWICHES & BURGERS RECIPES 73

Air-fryer Cheeseburger Spring Rolls 73
Air Fryer Turkey Burgers 73
Air Fryer Hamburgers 73
Air Fryer Amazing Burgers 74
Air Fryer Club Sandwich 74
Turkey Burgers 75
Air Fryer Cheeseburger Bombs 75
Lentil Veggie Burger Recipe 76
Frozen Hamburgers In The Air Fryer 77
Air Fryer Frozen Turkey Burgers 77

VEGETABLE & & VEGETARIAN RECIPES 78

Crispy Air Fryer Roasted Sprouts 78
Air Fryer Primavera Roasted Vegetables ... 78
Air Fryer Onion Rings 79
Cheesy Vegetarian 'sausage' Rolls 79
Air Fryer Broccoli And Carrots 80
Air Fryer Baked Potatoes 80
Air Fryer Roasted Potatoes Recipe 80
Vortex Stuffed Mushrooms 81
Air Fryer Cauliflower With Garlic 81
Air Fryer Roasted Asparagus 82
Air Roasted Asparagus 82
Crispy Air Fryer Brussels Sprouts 82
Steamed Veggies 83
Popcorn Vegan Pieces With Sauce 83
Instant Pot & Vortex Smashed Potatoes ... 84
Mashed Potato Balls 84
Air Fryer Baby Carrots 85
Air Fryer Veggie Chip Medley 85
Air Fryer Baked Potato 86
Air Fryer Grilled Tomato And Cheese 86
Easy Air Fryer Baked Potatoes 87
Cauliflower Buffalo Bites 87
Garlic Mashed Potatoes 87
Air Fryer Tofu 88

FAVORITE AIR FRYER RECIPES 89

Crispy Peanut Tofu With Squash Noodles 89
Mama Sue's Salsa 89
Air Fryer Pizza Recipe 90
Air Fryer Stuffed Jalapenos 90
Salami Chips 91
Frozen Potstickers In The Air Fryer 91

4

Air-fryer Katsu Bites	91	Air Fryer Biscuit Dough Pizzas	95
Pepperoni Pizza Bites	92	Air Fryer Italian Sausage	95
Dutch Baby	92	Air Fryer Mac & Cheese	96
Air Fryer Churro Bites	93	Air Fryer Butternut Squash Soup	96
Homemade Garlic Aioli	93	Air Fryer Sausage Recipe	97
Air Fryer Frozen Mozzarella Sticks	93	Smoked Sausage In The Air Fryer	97
Air Fryer Halloumi	94	Air Fryer Fried Rice	97
Air Fryer Acorn Squash	94	3 Ingredient Dog Treats	98
Air Fryer Hot Dogs	95	Air Fryer Frozen Dumplings	98

SNACKS & APPETIZERS RECIPES 99

Homemade Air Fryer Tater Tots	99	Air Fryer Zucchini Chips	104
Air Fryer Frozen French Fries	99	Air Fryer Crunchy Chickpeas	104
Air-fryer Pickle Chips	99	Air Fryer Truffle Fries	104
Air Fryer Avocado Fries	100	Air Fryer Potato Chips	105
Air Fryer Home Fries	101	Air Fryer Roasted Butternut Squash	106
Air Fryer Green Beans	101	Air Fryer Flower Fries	106
Air Fryer Sweet Potato Fries	101	Crispy Air Fryer French Fries	107
Air Fryer French Fries	102	Air Fryer Fried Pickles	107
Homemade Oven Chips	102	Air Fryer Carrot Fries	108
Air Fryer Pasta Chips	103	Air Fryer Roasted Chickpeas	108
Air Fryer Frozen Onion Rings	103	Air Fryer Kale Chips	109
Air Fryer Chips	104		

INTRODUCTION

Air fryers are full of hot air, and that's what is great about them. They are basically small, powerful ovens, and ovens use air as a vehicle for heat, whereas deep frying uses fat as the vehicle for heat. Because air fryers are ovens and not fryers, foods that come out of your air fryer will not be 100% identical to the onion rings at Cone-n-Shake or the calamari rings at your favorite bar and grill. The upshot is that air fryers are much less messy and oil-intensive than deep-frying. Even better, these lil' ovens can do much more than crank out faux fried food. Air fryers bring beautifully browned vegetables, crackly-skinned chicken wings, and even light and airy cakes, all within your reach.

HOW AIR FRYERS WORK

Your air fryer is like an amazing convection oven. It's small, yet mighty, and you can roast, broil, or bake in it. You cannot deep fry in it. Need a refresher on convection cooking? No problem.

Heat rises, so in a regular oven the top rack is always the hottest spot, which leads to uneven doneness. (It's also why a lot of cookie recipes tell you to rotate baking sheets from top to bottom and back to front midway through baking.) In a convection oven, however, fans blow hot air around so the temperature is equalized throughout the oven. Air fryers aren't *exactly* like convection ovens; their airflow is designed to more closely replicate the heat distribution of deep-frying in hot fat. But for our purposes, the convection oven analogy is good enough.

IMPORTANT TIPS TO KEEP IN MIND

1. Always have the grate in the basket. This allows hot air to circulate around the food, and also keeps the food from sitting in excess oil.
2. Air fryers are loud. When it's running, you'll hear whirring fans.
3. It's hands-on. Even browning requires you to remove the basket and shuffle the food around every few minutes.
4. It's fine to pull out the basket for a peek. You can do this at any point into the cooking process. No need to shut off the machine, as it shuts itself off when the basket is out.
5. Accordingly, make sure the drawer is pushed all the way in, or it won't turn back on. You'll know, because the air fryer will be suddenly quiet.
6. Food cooks fast, faster than you're used to! It's one of the best attributes of the air fryer. Your air fryer's manual likely has a handy table of cooking times and temperatures for common foods. The less food in the basket, the shorter the cook time will be; the more food, the longer it will be.
7. You may need a slightly lower temperature. A lot of air fryer recipes call for lower temperature settings than their conventional counterparts. This might seem fishy, but just go with it. Once again, air fryers get hot very fast and move that hot air around, so a slightly lower temperature will help keep food from getting too dark or crispy on the outside, while still being properly cooked on the inside.

MISTAKES TO AVOID

1. **Don't be too generous with oil.** Use a light hand with that oil! Excess oil ends up in the drawer under the grate, but if there's too much buildup, it might smoke. Generally speaking, if there's already fat on the food (skin-on chicken, for example, or frozen fried food), you might not need to oil the food at all. Vegetables, however, benefit from a light coating of oil, because it helps make them nice and brown.
2. **Don't grease the drawer with cooking spray.** Seems like that would be a good idea, right? But the baskets have nonstick coating, and cooking spray can damage the finish over time. (Really, it says so in the manual! What, didn't you read it?) In lieu of cooking spray, toss your food in oil instead—you're probably doing that already, in many cases—or rub it down with an oil-saturated paper towel. I found pre-fried frozen foods didn't need the help of extra grease.
3. **Don't crowd the drawer.** It's so tempting to add another handful of potato sticks or shaved beets, but you'll learn from experience that food comes out crisper and cooks up faster if you work in small batches.
4. **Don't neglect to shake the basket.** Doing this periodically ensures food is evenly exposed to heat, which gives you better browning. A lot of recipes call for you to shake the basket every five minutes. For larger items, like breaded fish fillets, flip them instead. If a recipe calls for shaking or flipping and you skip it, it's not detrimental, but it'll keep you from achieving that lucrative, oh-so-similar-to-fried-food result.
5. **Don't just dump the hot contents of the drawer into a bowl.** Use tongs or a spoon to get cooked food out. Excess oil collects under the removable grate in your basket, so if you yank out the basket and tip it onto a platter, the oil will come spilling out along with the grate. This can burn you, make a mess, and lead to greasy food.
6. **Don't trust the timer 100%.** A lot of basket-style air fryers have a dial you set like an old-fashioned kitchen timer, or like that kid's game Perfection. When the time's up it goes PING! and the machine stops. On one of the models I used, five minutes flew by suspiciously fast. So I set my phone's timer when I set the air fryer's timer, and guess what—the appliance was off by a few minutes. This is not a big deal; with air fryers, you just keep re-setting the timer until the food is done to your liking. But do realize that not all timers run accurately.
7. **Don't put the hot drawer on the countertop.** Think of the drawer as a hot pan. When you pull it from the unit, the bottom especially will be hot. Grab the drawer by the handle, not the other parts, and have a trivet or potholder ready to set it on if heat will damage your countertop.
8. **Don't get all touchy-feely with the air fryer.** The exterior of the air fryer can get hot (the back, likely). Not hot enough to burn you, but don't get all grabby with it.

HOW TO CLEAN YOUR AIR FRYER

It's important to clean your air fryer after every use, since a build-up of oil can make the unit smoke. In some instances, you can simply wipe off the drawer and grate with a paper towel. If they're gunky, hand wash. Most models have parts that are dishwasher safe, so check with your manual.

BREAKFAST & BRUNCH RECIPES

Air Fryer Breakfast Burritos

Servings: 6
Cooking Time: 5 Minutes

Ingredients:
- 6 medium flour tortillas
- 6 scrambled eggs
- ½ lb ground sausage – browned
- ½ bell pepper – minced
- ⅓ cup bacon bits
- ½ cup shredded cheese
- oil for spraying

Directions:
1. Combine the scrambled eggs, cooked sausage, bell pepper, bacon bits, and cheese in a large bowl. Stir to combine.
2. Spoon about a ½ cup of the mixture into the center of a flour tortilla.
3. Fold in the sides & then roll.
4. Repeat with the remaining ingredients.
5. Place the filled burritos into the air fryer basket & spray liberally with oil.
6. Cook at 330 degrees for 5 minutes or until hot and the tortilla is slightly cripsy.

Buttermilk Pancakes

Servings: 12

Ingredients:
- 2 cups (272 grams) all-purpose flour
- 3 tablespoons (42 grams) granulated sugar
- 1½ teaspoons (8 grams) baking powder
- 1½ teaspoons (8 grams) baking soda
- 1 teaspoon (5 grams) salt
- 2 cups (473 milliliters) buttermilk
- 2 eggs, lightly beaten
- ½ teaspoon (3 grams) vanilla extract
- 3 tablespoons (43 grams) unsalted butter, melted
- Unsalted butter or oil, for greasing

Directions:
1. Whisk the flour, sugar, baking powder, baking soda, and salt together in a bowl.
2. Add the buttermilk, eggs, vanilla extract, melted butter, and whisk until smooth—do not overmix. Let the batter rest at room temperature for 10 minutes.
3. Place the basket directly into the Smart Air Fryer basket, without the crisper plate.
4. Set temperature to 400°F and time to 5 minutes, then press Start/Pause to preheat.
5. Grease the bottom of the air fryer basket with butter or oil, being careful of hot surfaces.
6. Pour out the batter using ⅓ cup portions to form 2 pancakes on the bottom of the air fryer basket.
7. Set temperature to 340°F and time to 6 minutes, then press Start/Pause. Flip the pancakes halfway through cooking.
8. Remove the pancakes when done and repeat the cooking process with the remaining batter.
9. Serve warm.

Leftover Turkey Pot Pie

Ingredients:
- 3 Tbsp butter
- 3 Tbsp all-purpose flour
- 2 cups chicken broth
- 1 1/2 tsp herbs de Provence
- 1 1/2 tsp onion powder
- 1 tsp garlic powder
- 1/2 tsp salt
- 1/2 tsp black pepper
- 1 1/2 cups leftover turkey
- 10 oz frozen mixed vegetables
- 1/4 cup cream cheese
- 4 Grands Southern Homestyle Biscuits

Directions:
1. In a large, non-stick skillet, melt the butter over medium high heat. Whisk in the flour and cook for a minute or two to create a roux.

2. Whisk in the chicken broth until smooth and the mixture starts to thicken.
3. Stir in the herbs de Provence, onion powder, garlic powder, salt and pepper.
4. Stir in the turkey and vegetables. Simmer for a few minutes, stirring often.
5. Turn off heat and stir in the cream cheese until well incorporated.
6. Divide the pot pie mixture between four ceramic ramekin dishes. Top each dish with a biscuit.
7. Place the filled dishes into the air fryer oven.
8. Cook the pot pies at 320°F for 12 minutes, or until the biscuits are browned and cooked through. Enjoy!

Air Fryer Tex Mex Egg Rolls

Servings: 20
Cooking Time: 11 Minutes

Ingredients:
- 1 pound lean ground beef
- 1 onion finely diced
- 1 green pepper diced
- 1 package taco seasoning plus water as per package
- 2 tablespoons salsa
- 20 egg roll wrappers mine were 5"x5"
- 2 cups cheese shredded and divided (cheddar, Monterey jack, tex mex blend all work well). Cheese sticks also work great.
- oil for frying optional

Directions:
1. Brown ground beef and onions until no pink remains.
2. Stir in green peppers, taco seasoning, salsa, and water (as required on the seasoning package). Cook until the water evaporates.
3. Lay out each egg roll wrapper (in a diamond facing you). Place 1 ½ tablespoons each of cheese and taco filling in the center of each wrapper.
4. Fold diagonally, fold sides in and roll up sealing the tip with a little bit of the water. Brush the outside of each egg roll with a little bit of vegetable oil or spray with cooking spray.
5. Place in the air fryer basket 3-4 at a time and cook at 390°F for 8 minutes. Flip and cook for an additional 3 minutes.

Notes
To Deep Fry Egg Rolls in Oil:
Preheat oil to 350°F.
Carefully fry each egg roll for about 4-5 minutes or until browned and crispy.
Remove and place on a paper towel-lined paper to cool slightly before serving.
CAUTION: It is very important to make sure the wrappers are fully sealed when deep frying. Any ingredients that leak out have the chance to cause splattering which can cause severe burns.
To Make in the Oven:
Assemble taco egg rolls, spray with cooking spray.
Place in a single layer on a parchment-lined baking sheet.
Bake at 350°F until brown and crispy, flipping halfway through baking.

Spice Empanadas

Servings: 12

Ingredients:
- 1 tablespoon olive oil
- 1 cup sweet potato, grated
- ¼ cup yellow onion, grated
- 1 carrot, grated
- 3 garlic cloves, minced
- 1 can diced tomatoes (15 ounces)
- ½ pound ground beef
- 1 tablespoon parsley, chopped
- Empanada Dough
- 3 cups all-purpose flour, plus more for dusting surface
- ½ teaspoon kosher salt
- 10 tablespoons unsalted butter, softened to room temperature
- Items Needed
- Food Processor
- Rolling pin
- Pastry brush

- ¼ cup green olives, chopped
- ¼ cup pine nuts
- 2 teaspoons kosher salt
- ½ teaspoon ground cinnamon
- ½ teaspoon ground coriander
- ½ teaspoon ground cloves
- Chimichurri, for serving
- 2 large eggs
- Chimichurri, for serving
- Water, as needed

Directions:
1. Warm the olive oil in a large sauté pan over medium-high heat. Add the sweet potato, onions, and carrot and cook for 3–4 minutes, stirring often, until the potatoes and carrots are softened.
2. Add the garlic and tomatoes and stir to combine, then stir in the beef and break the beef apart with a spoon or spatula until it is browned and cooked through.
3. Stir in the remaining ingredients to the beef mixture, then simmer for 10 minutes or until most of the moisture has cooked off. Remove the pan from the heat to let cool slightly.
4. Place the flour and salt into the bowl of a food processor and pulse to combine, then add the butter and pulse several times.Blend in the egg and water a little bit at a time until the dough comes together and forms a shaggy dough
5. Turn the dough out onto a lightly floured surface and bring it together using your hands, adding more water as needed, a tiny bit at a time. The dough will be ready to use when it is smooth and not sticky but not crumbly or dry. Refrigerate wrapped in plastic wrap until ready to use.
6. Remove the dough from the refrigerator, divide the dough into portions, and keep them covered until ready to use.
7. Whisk an egg and 1 tablespoon of water together in a small bowl to make an egg wash.
8. Roll the dough portions out to ¼ to ⅛-inch-thick rounds using a rolling pin on a floured surface. Fill each dough round with 2 tablespoons of the filling, then fold the dough over the filling.
9. Fold the edges of the dough over each other starting at one end and ending at the other to seal. Alternatively, press the edges of the dough together with the tines of a fork to seal.
10. Brush the tops of the empanadas with the egg wash.
11. Select the Preheat function on the Air Fryer, adjust temperature to 375°F, then press Start/Pause.
12. Place the empanadas into the air fryer basket.
13. Set temperature to 375°F and time to 8 minutes, then press Start/Pause.
14. Remove the empanadas when done and brush again lightly with the egg wash for shine while they are still very hot, then serve with the chimichurri on the side.

Air-fryer Hash Brown
Servings: 4
Cooking Time: 20 Minutes

Ingredients:
- 500g brushed potatoes, peeled, grated
- 1 tsp onion powder
- 2 tbs extra virgin olive oil
- 5ml olive oil cooking spray
- 1/3 cup Greek-style yoghurt (to serve)
- 1/4 cup small continental parsley leaves (to serve)

Directions:
1. Preheat air fryer to 170°C for 2 minutes.
2. Place potato in a large clean tea towel and squeeze out as much moisture as possible. Place potato in a large bowl with onion powder and extra virgin olive oil, then stir to combine. Season with pepper.
3. Lightly spray air-fryer basket with oil. Spoon potato mixture into basket and press with a spatula to form a 1.5cm-thick round. Slide pan and basket into air fryer. Set timer for 20 minutes, turning hash brown

halfway through cooking, or until golden. Stand for 10 minutes, then transfer to a board. Serve topped with yoghurt
4. and parsley

Scallion Pancake
Servings: 8

Ingredients:
- 1/4 c. low-sodium soy sauce
- 2 tbsp. rice vinegar
- 2 tsp. sambal-style chili paste
- 1 tsp. sugar
- 1 2-inch piece fresh ginger, peeled and cut into matchsticks
- 1 14-oz pkg. round dumpling wrappers
- 1/4 c. toasted sesame oil
- 8 scallions, chopped (1 1/2 cups)
- 8 tbsp. canola oil

Directions:
1. In small bowl, whisk together soy sauce, rice vinegar, chili paste, and sugar; stir in ginger and set aside.
2. On cutting board, place 1 dumpling wrapper. Light brush top with sesame oil and scatter 2 teaspoons scallions on top. Top with second dumpling wrapper, pressing to adhere. Repeat with sesame oil, scallions, and wrappers until you have a stack of 6 wrappers. Repeat with remaining ingredients to make a total of 8 stacks of 6 wrappers each.
3. Working with 1 at a time, using a rolling pin, roll out each stack of wrappers to 6-inch-diameter circle, turning and flipping over as necessary. Repeat until all stacks are rolled out.
4. Heat 1 Tbsp canola oil in medium skillet on medium. Cook 1 pancake at a time until golden brown, 1 to 2 minutes per side. Repeat with remaining oil and pancake stacks. Serve sprinkled with any remaining scallions and with ginger-chili sauce for dipping.
5. AIR FRYER SHORTCUT SCALLION PANCAKES: Follow steps 1-2 (do not roll out stacks of wrappers). Heat air fryer to 400°F. Brush both sides of stacks liberally with canola oil. Place 4 stacks in air-fryer basket, spacing apart so they don't touch. Air-fry 3 to 4 minutes. Using tongs, flip and air-fry until golden brown and crispy, 3 to 4 minutes more. Repeat with remaining stacks. Sprinkle pancakes with more scallions and serve with ginger-chili sauce for dipping.

Air Fryer French Onion Tarts
Servings: 2
Cooking Time: 30 Minutes

Ingredients:
- 2 sheets shortcrust pastry, just thawed
- 1 tbsp olive oil
- 1 small brown onion, thinly sliced
- 75g cream cheese
- 2 tbsp sour cream
- 25g (¼ cup) grated cheddar
- 3 large eggs
- Chopped fresh chives, to serve (optional)
- Select all ingredients

Directions:
1. Lightly grease two 15cm fluted tartlet tins.
2. Place 1 sheet of pastry on a lightly floured bench. Top with the remaining pastry sheet. Sprinkle with a little flour and roll out to 3mm thickness. Cut in half diagonally. Ease 1 half into 1 prepared tart tin. Repeat with remaining pastry half and tart tin. Trim excess pastry. Line the pastry cases with baking paper and fill with pastry weights or rice. Place in the basket of an XXL airfryer and air fry at 200C for 6 minutes. Remove the paper and baking beans or rice and and air fry for a further 2 minutes.
3. Meanwhile, heat the oil in a frying pan over medium heat. Add onion and cook, stirring occasionally, for 10 minutes or until golden and caramelised. Set aside to cool slightly.
4. Combine cream cheese, sour cream, cheddar and 1 egg in a bowl. Add the onion. Stir to combine. Season. Divide the mixture

between tart cases. Make a small well in the centre of 1 tart. Crack an egg into the well. Repeat with remaining tart and egg. Season with pepper.
5. Air fry at 170C for 10-12 minutes or until just cooked. Leave in the air fryer to cool for 5 minutes or until the egg is cooked to your liking.
6. Sprinkle with chives, if using, to serve.

Air Fryer Pierogies With Onions
Servings: 2
Cooking Time: 22 Minutes

Ingredients:
- 14 frozen pierogies
- 1 small onion
- 1 tablespoon oil
- small pinch of sugar
- spraying oil

Directions:
1. Heat a large pot halfway full with water on high heat to a boil. Once boiling, cook pierogies for 5 minutes and remove from water/drain.
2. While water is heating up, slice the onion into long slices.
3. Place oil in an air fryer pan and cook on 300 for 1 minute.
4. Add onion to the pan, mix to coat, and cook on 300 degrees for 12-15 minutes, stirring every 3 minutes. Add a small pinch of sugar to them after cooking for 6 minutes and mix to coat.
5. Remove from the air fryer and set aside.
6. Place pierogies in an air fryer and cook at 350 degrees for 4 minutes.
7. Spritz the tops with oil and increase the temperature to 400. Cook for another 4-5 minutes until tops are golden brown.
8. Combine pierogies and onions and enjoy immediately.

Air Fryer Poached Eggs
Servings: 4
Cooking Time: 6 Minutes

Ingredients:
- 4 eggs
- olive oil
- water 3 tbsp per egg

Directions:
1. Preheat the air fryer to 370 degrees F for 3 minutes.
2. Lightly spray each ramekin with olive oil.
3. Add 3 tablespoons of hot water to each ramekin, then crack an egg into each ramekin, over the water.
4. Place ramekins in the air fryer basket. Air fry at 370 degrees F for 6-8 minutes, until the yolk ofegg reaches your desired doneness.
5. When eggs are done, use a rubber spatula or spoon to gently slide the eggs out of the ramekins.
6. Season with salt and pepper as desired.

NOTES
Variations
Change how you use the egg - While you can eat this perfect recipe right out of the ramekin, you can also use it to pair with other foods as well. If you make the egg sunny side up, it's so good to put on top of crispy vegetables or even a mound of homemade sweet potato hash. You can make this part of a healthy breakfast, or it can be a great option for lunch or dinner, too.

Don't forget that avocado toast is super popular and an easy hack for making a super trendy dish. Add toppings - If you want to take this egg mixture and change it up, you can add a few toppings! A creamy hollandaise sauce is a great idea, or you can add some salt and pepper to the oozy yolk. This egg recipe is really versatile in how you want to eat, and serve it, and that makes it one of the best food hacks out there.

Air Fryer Hard Boiled Eggs

Servings: 4
Cooking Time: 13 Minutes

Ingredients:
- 4 large eggs

Directions:
1. Preheat the air fryer to 300°F and carefully set the eggs in the basket.
2. Cook the eggs for 8-9 minutes for soft-boiled, 9-11 minutes for jammy eggs, and 11-13 minutes for hard-boiled eggs.
3. Remove the eggs from the air fryer and immediately place them in an ice water bath for 5 minutes.
4. Peel the eggs and enjoy.

Tips & Notes

You can add more than 4 large eggs to the air fryer if space allows. Just be sure the eggs aren't touching.

Every air fryer is different. You may have to test out your air fryer to master exactly how you like your eggs.

Reuben Egg Rolls

Servings: 6
Cooking Time: 10 Minutes

Ingredients:
- 6 egg roll wrappers
- 6 slices corned beef
- 6 slices swiss cheese cut into 1" strips
- 1 ¼ cups sauerkraut drained and squeezed dry
- 1 teaspoon caraway seeds optional
- 1 cup Thousand Island Dressing divided use
- oil for frying or air frying

Directions:
1. Preheat oil to 375°F or air fryer to 380°F.
2. Stack corned beef and cut into thin strips.
3. Lay egg roll wrappers with a corner pointed toward you. Divide corned beef, swiss cheese, and sauerkraut over the wrappers. Drizzle each with 1 tablespoon of the dressing and sprinkle with caraway seeds if using.
4. Dip your finger in water and run it along the edges of the egg roll wrapper.
5. Fold the two sides in and tightly roll the egg roll. Seal the edges.
6. If air frying, brush each egg roll with vegetable oil (or spray with cooking spray) and place in a single layer, seam side down. See below for oven or deep fryer instructions.
7. Cook 7 minutes. Flip and cook an additional 3-5 minutes or until crispy. Serve with remaining dressing for dipping.

Notes

To Bake in the Oven: Place egg rolls on a baking sheet sprayed with pan release at 350° F for 8 minutes. Flip them over and bake until they are browned, another 5-7 minutes.

To Deep Fry preheat oil to 350°F. Gently place egg rolls in preheated oil turning as needed until browned and crispy, about 4-5 minutes.

Egg Rolls can be prepared up to 2 days in advance and refrigerated or frozen. If cooking from frozen, add 2-3 minutes cooking time depending on the method used.

Air Fryer Chunky Monkey French Toast

Servings: 4
Cooking Time: 8 Minutes

Ingredients:
- 1.5 tablespoons melted coconut oil
- 3 large eggs
- ¼ cup milk any kind
- 2 tablespoons mashed ripe banana
- 2 tablespoons maple syrup
- ¼ teaspoon ground cinnamon
- 1 tablespoon drippy peanut butter
- Pinch salt
- 4 slices sourdough bread
- ¼ cup chopped chocolate pieces
- 2 tablespoons chopped salted and roasted walnuts
- 1 banana sliced into rounds
- 1.5 tablespoons melted coconut oil

Directions:
1. Preheat the air fryer to 370°F and add the melted coconut oil to the bottom of the air fryer.
2. Whisk the eggs in a large bowl and then add the milk, mashed banana, maple syrup, cinnamon, peanut butter, and salt to the eggs and whisk until combined. Pour the egg mixture into a baking dish or pan.
3. Dip each piece of bread into the egg mixture. Flipping the bread over and allowing the egg mixture to soak into the bread.
4. Place two slices of french toast in the air fryer and cook the french toast for 4 minutes on each side until golden brown. Remove the french toast from the air fryer and sprinkle the chocolate over the hot french toast, so it softens. Top the chocolate with chopped walnuts and sliced bananas.
5. Repeat step 4 with the other pieces of french toast.

Tips & Notes
Some air fryers may be able to fit all four pieces of french toast.
This recipe is based on Ben & Jerry's ice cream flavor. If you want different toppings, go for it.
It was helpful to use a metal spatula to flip the french toast over.

Five Cheese Pull Apart Bread

Ingredients:
- 1 bread loaf, medium
- 7 tbsp butter
- 2 tsp garlic puree
- ½ cup cheddar cheese
- 4 oz. goat cheese
- ½ cup mozzarella cheese
- ½ cup Gouda cheese
- 4 oz. brie cheese
- 2 tsp chives
- salt and pepper, to taste

Directions:
1. Grate your hard cheese into 3 different piles and set aside.
2. In a saucepan, melt the butter on medium heat. Add in the chives, salt, pepper and garlic. Cook for another 2 minutes, mix well and then set aside.
3. Using a bread knife, create little slits into your bread. In each of the little slits cover with the garlic butter mixture until they are all covered. Then, insert the goat and brie cheese in all of the slits to give them a lovely creamy taste.
4. Spread the cheddar, mozzarella and Gouda cheese over the tops and fill the cracks with them. Place your standard rack in the air fryer and place the bread on top. Air fry it at 350° for 4 minutes, or until the cheese is melted and the bread is warm.

Tinga Cauliflower Tacos
Servings: 3

Ingredients:
- 2 small or 1 large cauliflower, greens removed and set aside, cut into small florets
- 2 tbsp olive oil
- 1 tsp dried oregano
- 1 tsp chipotle powder
- Salt and pepper
- For the sauce
- 450g vine tomatoes, stems removed and washed
- 3 cloves garlic, with skin smashed to loosen skin
- 1/2 red or white onion, whole
- 2 tbsp chipotle paste
- 1 tsp brown sugar
- 1 tbsp fresh lime juice
- Salt and pepper
- For the slaw
- Greens from cauliflower, washed and shredded
- 5 radish, sliced thinly
- 150g red cabbage, shredded
- 1 spring onion
- 1 red or green chilli
- 2 tbsp vegan mayo
- 1-2 tbsp fresh lime juice

- 5g fresh coriander, chopped
- 1/2 tsp brown sugar
- To taste salt and pepper
- To serve
- Pack fresh corn tortillas
- Guacamole
- Salsa
- Vegan sour cream
- Chillies
- COOKING MODE
- When entering cooking mode - We will enable your screen to stay 'always on' to avoid any unnecessary interruptions whilst you cook!

Directions:
1. Toss all the ingredients together for the cauliflower, you will need to cook this in two batches
2. Place ½ ingredients for cauliflower in drawer 1. Turn on the Ninja Foodi Dual Zone Air Fryer, select "1", select "AIR FRY", set the temperature to 180 and the time to 10-12 minutes
3. Place the tomatoes, garlic and onion in to drawer 2. Select "2", press "ROAST ", set the time to 15 minutes and the temp to 200C. Press "SYNC" and then "Start"
4. When sauce is done remove and place in a food processor with chipotle paste, brown sugar, lime juice and set it to chop
5. Add the rest of cauliflower in to drawer 1 of the Ninja Foodi Dual Zone Air Fryer. Select "1", select "AIR FRY", set the temperature to 180 and the time to 10-12 minutes
6. Add the tortillas to drawer 2 , select "2", select "BAKE", set the temperature to 180 and the time to 2-3 minutes. Press "SYNC" and select "Start"
7. Once the cauliflower is all cooked, toss with ¾ of sauce and ROAST at 180 for 5 minutes to warm through, toss as it cooks. Toss remaining through once heated to be sure it is nice and saucy
8. Toss all ingredients together for slaw
9. Serve on tortillas with slaw and guacamole and salsa, vegan sour cream

Air Fryer Hand Pies

Ingredients:
- 2 Fuji apples, peeled, cored, and cut into 1/4-inch dice (2 cups)
- 3/4 cup raspberries
- 2 tbsp light brown sugar, lightly packed
- 1 tbsp granulated sugar, plus additional for sprinkling
- 1/4 tsp ground cinnamon
- pinch kosher salt
- 1 tbsp apple juice or cider
- 1-1/2 tsp cornstarch mixed with 1 tsp water (slurry)
- 1 package (2 rounds) refrigerated pie crusts
- 1 large egg yolk mixed with 1 tsp water (egg wash)

Directions:
1. In a medium pot, stir together apples, raspberries, sugars, cinnamon, salt, and apple juice or cider. Bring to a simmer over medium heat, cover, and reduce heat to low. Cook, stirring occasionally, until apples begin to soften but still retain their shape, about 15 mins.
2. Add the slurry to the filling mixture. Increase heat to medium and cook for 1-2 mins, until thickened. Remove from heat and cool to room temperature.
3. While the filling is cooling, unroll pie crusts. Cut the dough into 4-inch circles using a cookie cutter, re-rolling the scraps as needed. You'll need 12 circles.
4. Place 1 tbsp of filling on the center of each circle. Brush the edges of the dough with water, fold the dough in half over the filling, and press to seal. Don't overfill.
5. Use a fork to crimp the sealed edges. Lightly brush the pies with egg wash and use the tip of a paring knife to pierce two small slits in the top of each pie. Sprinkle the tops with sugar.
6. Preheat KRUPS air fryer to 320°F. Add the pies in a single layer, 6 at a time, and bake for 15 minutes, until the tops are golden. (Refrigerate the pies that aren't being

baked so the dough doesn't become too soft.) Remove to a wire rack to cool.
7. Repeat with the remaining pies and enjoy!

Air Fryer French Toast Sticks

Servings: 4
Cooking Time: 8 Minutes

Ingredients:
- 4-6 pieces bread (allow it to sit out for 2-3 hours before using)
- 2 eggs
- 3 tbsp granulated white sugar
- 2 tsp cinnamon

Directions:
1. Mix the cinnamon and sugar together in a small bowl or plate and set aside.
2. Stack the bread and then use a serated knife to cut the slices into thirds.
3. Whisk the eggs together and pour them into a rimmed plate.
4. Dip the bread pieces into the egg and then dip into the cinnamon and sugar.
5. Place the bread into the prepared Air Fryer basket in a single layer with an inch or two between slices.
6. Air Fryer the bread pieces for 8-9 minutes on 370 degrees Fahrenheit, flipping them halfway through.
7. Remove from the Air Fryer and serve immediately.

Steamed Cinnamon Buns

Servings: 10
Cooking Time: 36 Minutes

Ingredients:
- 2 cups flour
- ¼ cup luke warm water
- 1 pkt instant yeast
- 10ml sugar
- 90ml warm milk
- 40ml vegetable oil
- 5ml Vanilla essence
- 1tsp salt
- ½ cup soft butter
- 1 tsp cinnamon
- ½ cup dark brown sugar
- ¼ cup chopped pecan nuts (optional)
- Topping
- ½cup icing sugar
- 1 Tbsp water

Directions:
1. Mix the yeast & sugar into the lukewarm water and set aside until it begins to bubble.
2. Sift the flour into a large bowl.
3. Mix the milk, oil, vanilla essence and salt together.
4. Pour into the flour and mix well turn out onto a floured surface and knead until the mixture is smooth.
5. Place in a bowl and cover with cling film or a damp cloth until it has doubled in size.
6. Remove from the bowl and knead then roll out into a rectangle about 5cm thick.
7. Mix the cinnamon, sugar & pecan nuts together.
8. Spread the soft butter over the dough and then sprinkle with cinnamon and sugar mix.
9. Roll up and cut into 10cm pieces.
10. Grease and line the springform tin and place the cut buns in the tin with 1cm spaces between each bun.
11. Cover the pan with foil.
12. Pour 1 cup of water in the base of the Instant Pot place the Trivet into the Instant Pot and place the cake tin on the Trivet.
13. Close the Instant Pot lid and set to Pressure Cook on High for 15mins.
14. Allow a Natural Pressure Release.
15. Remove from the Instant Potand remove the foil.
16. Place in the Vortex basket and set to bake at 180C degrees for 6 mins.
17. For the topping mix the icing sugar and water together add more water if needed.
18. Pour over the buns when they have cooled slightly.
19. Enjoy with whipped cream and roast apricots.

Air Fryer Egg Rolls

Servings: 12-14
Cooking Time: 10 Minutes

Ingredients:
- Kosher salt
- 1/2 small head of cabbage, cored and thinly sliced
- 2 medium carrots, julienned
- 2 stalks celery, julienned
- Ice
- 3 tbsp. low-sodium soy sauce
- 2 tbsp. hoisin
- 2 tbsp. oyster sauce
- 2 tsp. toasted sesame oil
- 1 tbsp. vegetable or other neutral oil, plus more for brushing
- 2 cloves garlic, minced
- 1 tsp. minced fresh ginger
- 1 lb. ground pork
- Freshly ground black pepper
- 12 to 14 egg roll wrappers
- Hot Chinese mustard and duck sauce, for serving

Directions:
1. In a large pot, bring 4 quarts salted water to a boil. Add cabbage, carrots, and celery and cook until slightly softened, about 2 minutes. Transfer to an ice bath.
2. Once cool enough to handle, drain and squeeze veggies with a kitchen towel until water is removed; set aside.
3. In a small bowl, combine soy sauce, hoisin, oyster sauce, and sesame oil.
4. In a large skillet over medium-high heat, heat vegetable oil until shimmering. Cook garlic and ginger, stirring, until fragrant, about 30 seconds. Add pork and cook, breaking up with a spoon, until browned and starting to crisp, 4 to 5 minutes.
5. Drain fat from skillet until about 1 tablespoon remains. Add soy sauce mixture and toss pork to coat. Cook over medium-high heat, stirring, 1 minute. Add veggies and cook, stirring, until combined and warmed through, 2 to 3 minutes more; season with salt and black pepper. Let cool slightly.
6. On a clean work surface, arrange an egg roll wrapper in a diamond shape. Spoon 2 heaping tablespoons filling onto bottom third of wrapper. Fold up bottom half and tightly fold in sides. Gently roll and seal edges with a couple drops of water, pressing to adhere.
7. Working in batches, generously brush egg rolls with vegetable oil. In an air-fryer basket, arrange egg rolls in a single layer. Cook at 400°, flipping halfway through, until golden brown and crispy, about 10 minutes.
8. Serve egg rolls with mustard and duck sauce alongside.

Air Fryer Falafel

Servings: 16
Cooking Time: 15 Minutes

Ingredients:
- 2 cups dried chickpeas (NOT canned or cooked chickpeas)
- 1 cup red onion, chopped
- 6 garlic cloves, peeled
- 1 cup fresh parsley, leaves and tender stems
- ½ cup fresh cilantro, leaves and tender stems
- ¼ cup fresh dill, stems removed
- 2 teaspoons ground cumin
- 2 teaspoons ground coriander
- 1 teaspoon sea salt, or to taste
- 1 teaspoon black pepper
- ½ teaspoon red pepper flakes (optional)
- 1 ½ tablespoons toasted sesame seeds (optional)
- 1 teaspoon baking powder (optional)
- SERVE WITH: Pita bread, tahini sauce, hummus, tomatoes, cucumber, lettuce, lemon wedges

Directions:
1. The day before you plan to cook the falafel, place the dried chickpeas in a large bowl. Fill the bowl with water, covering the

chickpeas by at least 2 inches. Soak for 18-24 hours until softened, then drain the chickpeas well and pat them dry.
2. Add the chickpeas, onion, garlic, herbs, and spices to the bowl of a food processor fitted with a blade. Pulse for 30 seconds, scrape down the sides of the bowl, then process again for 20-30 more seconds until well combined.
3. Transfer the mixture to a bowl, cover it tightly with a lid or plastic wrap, and refrigerate for at least 1 hour or overnight.
4. When ready to cook, remove the bowl from the refrigerator and stir the sesame seeds and baking powder into the mixture.
5. Wet your hands, then scoop heaping tablespoonfuls of the mixture and form it into balls or patties (½ inch in thickness each).
6. Spray the inner basket of the air fryer with cooking spray, then place the falafel in an even layer inside, being sure not to overcrowd. Lightly spray the falafel with cooking spray as well.
7. Air fry at 380 degrees F for 15 minutes, flipping them once halfway through the cook time, until they're golden brown and crispy. Repeat with any remaining falafel balls.

NOTES
If your falafel batter feels loose and won't hold together, add 1 to 1 ½ tablespoons of chickpea flour or all-purpose flour to help bind it.

Air Fryer Bacon Cinnamon Rolls
Servings: 8
Cooking Time: 8 Minutes

Ingredients:
- 8 slices bacon
- 1 can refrigerated cinnamon rolls

Directions:
1. Place the bacon slices in the basket of the air fryer in a single layer. (It's ok if the bacon overlaps a little) Close the basket door and air fry at 380 degrees Fahrenheit for 8-10 minutes. Check the bacon after 8 minutes for doneness. Don't let it get too crispy or it will break when rolling.
2. While bacon is cooking, open cinnamon roll package, and separate dough. Reserve icing packet for later. If using homemade cinnamon roll dough, cut into 6 x 1-inch strips to use for this recipe.
3. When bacon is done, unroll each strip of dough. Place one to two strips of bacon on each piece of dough, and then re-roll the cinnamon roll into its original shape. Repeat with remaining cinnamon rolls.
4. Lightly spray the air fryer basket with nonstick cooking spray, or line with air fryer parchment paper. Place the cinnamon roll dough in the Air Fryer basket, leaving a little space in between each cinnamon roll.
5. Air fry at 360 degrees F for 6- 8 minutes to allow the cinnamon rolls to fully cook, until they are a golden brown color. If you want the tops to be a little crispier, consider adding an additional minute to the cook time.
6. Remove the cinnamon rolls from the Air Fryer and top the rolls with icing while they are still warm. Serve immediately. Top with powdered sugar or chocolate chips while warm, if using.

Air Fryer Cinnamon Rolls
Servings: 8
Cooking Time: 8 Minutes

Ingredients:
- For the dough
- 1 3/4 cups self rising flour
- 1 cup vanilla yogurt Greek, coconut, or soy
- For the filling
- 2 tablespoons butter melted
- 1/4 cup brown sugar * See notes
- 2 teaspoons cinnamon
- For the frosting
- 2 oz cream cheese softened ** See notes
- 2 tablespoons butter softened ** See notes
- 6 tablespoons powdered sugar *** See notes

Directions:
1. In a large mixing bowl, add the flour and yogurt and mix well, until combined. If the dough is too thick, add more yogurt. If the dough is too thin, add more flour.
2. Lightly flour a kitchen surface and transfer the dough on top. Gently knead it several times, before rolling out into a large rectangular shape, around 1/2 an inch in thickness.
3. In a small bowl, add the melted butter, brown sugar, and cinnamon. Using a spatula, spread the cinnamon mixture on top, reserving half an inch around the sides.
4. Beginning at the long end of the dough, tightly roll up the dough into a log. Use a sharp knife to slice the log into eight portions.
5. Place 3 or 4 of the cinnamon rolls into an air fryer basket lined with parchment paper. Air fry at 180C/350F for 7-8 minutes, until the edges are lightly golden brown.
6. Remove the cinnamon rolls from the air fryer basket. Add remaining cinnamon rolls and repeat the process until they are all air fried.
7. Let the cinnamon rolls cool slightly, before adding the frosting. To make the frosting, add the cream cheese and butter in a mixing bowl. Beat together until combined. Add the powdered sugar and mix until smooth.

Notes
* Coconut sugar, white sugar, or a brown sugar substitute work.
** Dairy free butter and cream cheese work.
*** Or sugar free powdered sugar.
TO STORE: Leftover air fried cinnamon rolls can be stored in the refrigerator, covered, for up to three days.
TO FREEZE: Place the rolls in an airtight container and store them in the freezer for up to two months.
TO REHEAT: Microwave the rolls for 20 seconds or reheat in the air fryer for 2-3 minutes.

Homemade Air Fryer Pizza Rolls
Servings: 8
Cooking Time: 15 Minutes

Ingredients:
- 1 can refrigerated pizza dough or 1 pound homemade pizza dough
- 1 cup pizza sauce divided
- 1 ½ cups mozzarella cheese shredded
- ⅓ cup parmesan cheese shredded
- ⅔ cup mini pepperoni or chopped pepperoni
- ½ teaspoon garlic powder

Directions:
1. Preheat air fryer to 330°F.
2. Roll pizza dough out to approximately 12" x 8". Spread ½ cup pizza sauce over top of the dough.
3. Top with mozzarella, parmesan cheese, and mini pepperoni. Roll dough cinnamon roll style.
4. Cut into 8 pieces and place in the air fryer (add a few extra pepperonis on top if desired). Pinch the bottom of each roll a little bit to seal in the cheese.
5. Bake for 11-14 minutes or until pizza rolls are browned and cooked through.
6. Serve with remaining pizza sauce for dipping.

Notes
Air Fryers can vary so your pizza rolls may need a few minutes more or less to cook through. Check them a little bit early the first time you make these to ensure they don't overcook.
If using 'toppings' that have a lot of moisture such as mushrooms or pineapple, they should be cooked and squeezed dry before adding. Crisp veggies (such as peppers and onions) are best pre-cooked.

Air Fryer Frozen Texas Toast

Servings: 4
Cooking Time: 10 Minutes

Ingredients:
- 4 Frozen Texas Toasts (Cheese or Garlic)
- chopped parsley ,optional
- EQUIPMENT
- Air Fryer

Directions:
1. Place the frozen Texas toasts in the air fryer basket and spread in an even layer (make sure they aren't overlapping). No oil spray is needed.
2. CHEESE TEXAS TOAST
3. Air Fry at 340°F/170°C for about 7-10 minutes, or until the cheese is golden and the toast is heated through. Top with optional chopped parsley if desired.
4. If you're cooking only 1-2 pieces it might take about 5-6 minutes. Timing will also depend on how crisp you like your toast, the type of cheese, how thick the toast is, etc. Test a piece first and you'll know more of what your preferred timing is like for your particular frozen cheese toast.
5. GARLIC TEXAS TOAST (NO CHEESE)
6. Air Fry at 340°F/170°C for 5 minutes. Flip the garlic bread over.
7. Continue to Air Fry at 340°F/170°C for another 1-5 minutes or until cooked to your desired golden crispness.Top with optional chopped parsley if desired.
8. If you're cooking only 1-2 pieces of garlic bread it might take about 5-6 minutes total time, depending on how crisp you like your toast. Test a piece first and you'll know more of what your preferred timing is like.

NOTES
Air Frying Tips and Notes:
No Oil Necessary. Cook Frozen - Do not thaw first.
Cook in a single layer in the air fryer basket.
Recipe timing is based on a non-preheated air fryer. If cooking in multiple batches back to back, the following batches may cook a little quicker.
Recipes were tested in 3.7 to 6 qt. air fryers. If using a larger air fryer, they might cook quicker so adjust cooking time.
If you're using an oven-style air fryer with racks, you will need to rotate the racks because the top racks closest to the heating element will cook much quicker.

Air Fryer Egg Bites

Servings: 6
Cooking Time: 10 Minutes

Ingredients:
- 6 large eggs
- 1 tbsp milk
- 4 slices bacon crumbled
- 1/2 cup cheddar cheese shredded
- 1/2 tsp salt
- 1/4 tsp pepper
- 1 green onion chopped

Directions:
1. In a large bowl, combine the eggs and milk, and whisk together.
2. Add in the crumbled bacon, grated cheddar cheese, onions, and seasonings, stirring to combine.
3. Equally divide the egg mixture into silicone cups, about ⅔ full, leaving room for them to rise.
4. Place in the air fryer basket, or on a baking sheet if you have tray air fryer.
5. Cook at 300 degrees F for 8-10 minutes.

DESSERTS RECIPES

Chocolate Chickpea Bites

Ingredients:
- 1 can of chickpeas (you can also use your Instant Pot to cook them from scratch)
- 1 tbsp cooking oil
- 1 slab dark chocolate of choice

Directions:
1. Heat your Vortex air fryer to 200°C and set the timer to 15 minutes.
2. Drain and rinse chickpeas. To get rid of excessive moisture, you can pat-dry using a paper towel.
3. Toss the chickpeas with your cooking oil of choice.
4. Dump the chickpeas in your Vortex air fryer drawer. Cook for 12-15 minutes, shaking a couple of times. When chickpeas are cooked to your liking, remove from air fryer and let them cool.
5. Melt your chocolate and add all of your chickpeas. Make sure they're all evenly coated with chocolate and spread them out on some baking paper.
6. Once set, enjoy!

Salted Caramel Snickerdoodle Skillet Cookie

Servings: 4

Ingredients:
- 2¾ cups all-purpose flour
- 2 teaspoons cream of tartar
- 1 teaspoon baking soda
- ½ teaspoon kosher salt
- 1 teaspoon ground cinnamon, plus more for serving
- 1½ cups granulated sugar
- 4 ounces unsalted butter, room temperature
- 1 teaspoon vanilla extract
- 2 large eggs
- ½ cup salted caramel, plus more for serving
- Vanilla ice cream, for serving
- Items Needed:
- Stand mixer fitted with paddle attachment
- Cast iron skillet (6-inch diameter) or cake pan

Directions:
1. Whisk the flour, cream of tartar, baking soda, salt, and cinnamon together in a medium bowl.
2. Cream the sugar and butter together in a stand mixer fitted with the paddle attachment, then add the vanilla extract.
3. Add the eggs, one at a time, until fully combined, scraping down the sides of the bowl as needed with a rubber spatula.
4. Add the dry ingredients to the stand mixer and beat on low just until combined. Add the salted caramel and stir to swirl it into the dough, but do not mix it in completely.
5. Fill the skillet or cake pan ⅔ full with dough. Reserve the remaining dough in the refrigerator for a second batch of cookies later.
6. Place the cooking pot into the base of the Indoor Grill, followed by the basket.
7. Select the Bake function, adjust temperature to 320°F and time to 20 minutes, then press Start/Pause to preheat.
8. Place the skillet or cake pan into the preheated basket, then close the lid.
9. Select the Broil function, adjust time 3 minutes, then press Start/Pause.
10. Remove the skillet or cake pan when done and let cool slightly.
11. Serve the cookie in slices, drizzled with salted caramel sauce, sprinkled with cinnamon, and a scoop of vanilla ice cream on top.

Homemade Cannoli

Servings: 20

Ingredients:
- FOR THE FILLING:
- 1 (16-oz.) container ricotta
- 1/2 c. mascarpone cheese

- 1/2 c. powdered sugar, divided
- 3/4 c. heavy cream
- 1 tsp. pure vanilla extract
- 1 tsp. orange zest
- 1/4 tsp. kosher salt
- 1/2 c. mini chocolate chips, for garnish
- FOR THE SHELLS:
- 2 c. all-purpose flour, plus more for surface
- 1/4 c. granulated sugar
- 1 tsp. kosher salt
- 1/2 tsp. cinnamon
- 4 tbsp. cold butter, cut into cubes
- 6 tbsp. white wine
- 1 large egg
- 1 egg white, for brushing
- Vegetable oil, for frying

Directions:
1. MAKE FILLING:
2. Drain ricotta by placing it a fine mesh strainer set over a large bowl. Let drain in refrigerator for at least an hour and up to overnight.
3. In a large bowl using a hand mixer, beat heavy cream and 1/4 cup powdered sugar until stiff peaks form.
4. In another large bowl, combine ricotta, mascarpone, remaining 1/4 cup powdered sugar, vanilla, orange zest, and salt. Fold in whipped cream. Refrigerate until ready to fill cannoli, at least 1 hour.
5. MAKE SHELLS:
6. In a large bowl, whisk together flour, sugar, salt, and cinnamon. Cut butter into flour mixture with your hands or pastry cutter until pea-sized. Add wine and egg and mix until a dough forms. Knead a few times in bowl to help dough come together. Pat into a flat circle, then wrap in plastic wrap and refrigerate at least 1 hour and up to overnight.
7. On a lightly floured surface, divide dough in half. Roll one half out to ⅛" thick. Use a 4" circle cookie cutter to cut out dough. Repeat with remaining dough. Re-roll scraps to cut a few extra circles.
8. Wrap dough around cannoli molds and brush egg whites where the dough will meet to seal together.
9. FOR FRYING:
10. In a large pot over medium heat, heat about 2" of oil to 360°. Working in batches, add cannoli molds to oil and fry, turning occasionally, until golden, about 4 minutes. Remove from oil and place on a paper towel-lined plate. Let cool slightly.
11. When cool enough to handle or using a kitchen towel to hold, gently twist shells off of molds to remove.
12. Place filling in a pastry bag fitted with an open star tip. Pipe filling into shells, then dip ends in mini chocolate chips.
13. FOR AIR FRYER:
14. Working in batches, place molds in basket of air fryer and cook at 350° for 12 minutes, or until golden.
15. When cool enough to handle or using a kitchen towel to hold, gently remove twist shells off of molds.
16. Place filling in a pastry bag fitted with an open star tip. Pipe filling into shells, then dip ends in mini chocolate chips.

Air Fryer Halloween Ghost Cupcakes

Servings: 24
Cooking Time: 30 Minutes

Ingredients:
- cake mix 15.25 oz
- 1 1/4 cups water
- 1/2 cup vegetable oil
- Topping
- 1 tub frosting
- 1 package candy eyes

Directions:
1. Air fry 350 degrees Fahrenheit 10-12 minutes. Makes 2 dozen cupcakes
2. Use a medium bowl, to combine the cake mix with water, vegetable oil, and eggs. (or according to your box mix directions) Stir,

or if using an electric mixer, beat on medium speed until creamy.
3. Once the batter is prepared, place the silicone liners in your air fryer basket.
4. Carefully pour the cupcake batter from the mixing bowl until they are about ¾ full. (You can use a cupcake tin with liners, if it will fit in your air fryer)
5. Air fry the cupcakes at 350 degrees Fahrenheit for 10-12 minutes.
6. Once done, remove from the air fryer basket and start the next batch. Be sure to allow the cupcakes to cool before frosting.
7. To top the cupcakes with your ghost frosting, add vanilla or buttercream on cupcake using a frosting bag. Going in a continual circular motion, continue to make a full circle, until you have a small mound of frosting, to create a ghost form.
8. Add the two edible eyes to each ghost to complete the face.

NOTES

Not all Air fryers are the same. Wattages can affect cooking time.

Having cake batter near the air fryer fan can blow the tops of the cupcakes just a bit.

Be careful not to fill the silicone liners to full or the batter will blow around in the air fryer.

If you can't find candy eyeballs, you can use black writing icing, a drop of black food gel, or mini chocolate chips for the eyes.

Air Fryer Berry Crisp

Servings: 2

Ingredients:
- FRUIT FILLING
- 1 c. fresh raspberries
- 3/4 c. fresh blueberries
- 1/2 c. fresh blackberries
- 2 tbsp. granulated sugar
- 2 tsp. ground flaxseeds
- 1/2 tsp. pure vanilla extract
- Pinch of kosher salt
- TOPPING
- 1/3 c. whole wheat flour
- 3 tbsp. old-fashioned rolled oats or chopped nuts, such as almonds or pecans
- 1 tbsp. granulated sugar
- Pinch of kosher salt
- 2 tbsp. butter, softened
- Olive oil cooking spray

Directions:
1. FRUIT FILLING
2. In a medium bowl, toss raspberries, blueberries, blackberries, sugar, flaxseeds, vanilla, and salt until coated.
3. Divide berry mixture between 2 (6") aluminum pie plates.
4. TOPPING
5. In a medium bowl, whisk flour, oats, sugar, and salt. Add butter and, using your hands, squeeze mixture together until clumps form.
6. Sprinkle topping over filling; generously spray with cooking spray. Place 1 pan in an air-fryer basket. Cook at 370° until filling is bubbly and top is golden, about 15 minutes. Let cool slightly. Repeat with remaining crisp.

Air Fryer Blueberry Hand Pies

Servings: 4
Cooking Time: 5 Minutes

Ingredients:
- 1 cup blueberries
- 8 ounces cream cheese
- 1 Tablespoon lemon juice
- ½ teaspoon lemon zest
- 1 roll dough refrigerated
- 1 egg
- 1 Tablespoon sweetened condensed milk

Directions:
1. Unroll the pie crust from the packaging onto a clean flat surface.
2. Use a pie cutter or a knife to cut 6 inch circles from the dough. Flatten and roll the dough as needed to get as many circles as you can from the packaged dough.

3. Combine the lemon juice and lemon zest with the cream cheese.
4. Stir the blueberries into the cream cheese mixture.
5. Add 1-2 tablespoons of the blueberry filling to one side of the dough.
6. Fold the dough over, and seal by pinching or using a fork on the edges.
7. Beat the egg in a small bowl and then combine it with the condensed milk to make the egg wash. Brush the pies with the egg-wash mixture.
8. Cut 3 small slits into the top of the pie crusts.
9. Prepare the air fryer basket if needed. Place the pies in a single layer in the bottom of the basket of the air fryer.
10. Air fry the pies at 380 degrees Fahrenheit for 6 minutes, flipping the pies halfway through the cooking time.

NOTES

If you have the perfect flaky pie crust recipe, use it! I like using already-made pie dough because it's easy and simple, but you can literally use anything that you want. Make a buttery crust, or use a puff pastry instead - options are always good.

For the best results, store leftovers in an airtight container in the fridge. You can then enjoy this easy blueberry hand pie recipe warm or cool the next day!

I love the taste of fresh fruit the best, but that doesn't mean that you can't use frozen fruit. This easy recipe is versatile, with easy steps that anyone can do.

Air Fryer Cream Cheese Cherry Pies

Servings: 4
Cooking Time: 6 Minutes

Ingredients:
- 12 ounces cherry pie filling
- 8 ounces cream cheese softened
- 1 egg beaten
- 1 pie crust rolled refrigerated dough

Directions:

1. Roll out the refrigerated pie dough on a cutting board and cut them into 6" dough circles.
2. Use a mini pie maker, round cookie cutter or a small plate as a template for the desired size.
3. In a medium-sized bowl mix the cherry pie filling and cream cheese together.
4. Whisk the egg in a separate shallow bowl.
5. Scoop 2 tablespoons of the cherry cream cheese mixture into the center of the dough circles.
6. Fold the circle in half, then use a fork to crimp the edges.
7. Spritz the air fryer basket with cooking spray.
8. Place pies in a single layer into the prepared air fryer basket, then brush each pie with the egg mixture.
9. Air fry the pies at 380 degrees F for 6 minutes, flipping the pies carefully halfway through the cooking process.
10. Remove pies and place them on baking racks so the pies remain crispy prior to serving.
11. Serve while warm.

NOTES

Optional Flavors: Vanilla extract, nutmeg, lemon zest, cinnamon, cardamom, almond extract or all spice.

Optional Toppings: Powdered sugar, granulated sugar, caramel sauce, cinnamon sugar, toasted coconut or a dollop of whipped cream.

Kitchen Tips: Use parchment paper liners if you do not have nonstick cooking spray.

NOTE: I make this recipe in my Cosori 5.8 qt. air fryer. Depending on your air fryer, size and wattages, the cook time may need to be adjusted 1-2 minutes.

Change things up! There are several flavors of canned filling that are available in your local grocery stores that you can use in this recipe. Some popular flavors are apple, raspberry, peach, strawberry and blueberry.

Air Fryer Strawberry Nutella Hand Pies

Servings: 4
Cooking Time: 5 Minutes

Ingredients:
- 1/2 cup strawberries sliced
- 2 Tablespoons hazelnut spread Nutella
- 1 pie dough refrigerated
- 1 egg whisked

Directions:
1. Unroll the pie dough and cut out the dough for each hand pie.
2. Top the pie dough with Nutella and sliced strawberries.
3. Cut little shapes into the dough if desired. Fold the dough over and use a fork to crimp and seal the edges.
4. Place the hand pies in a single layer in the air fryer basket and brush with egg.
5. Air fry hand pies at 380 degrees Fahrenheit for 5-6 minutes or until golden brown.
6. Carefully remove the pies from the air fryer and serve.

NOTES
To make these hand pies I use a little hand held pie maker. You don't need this to make them! You can use a bowl or plate as your guide and use a butter knife to cut around the edges.
Optional: I made these for Valentine's day so I cut cute little heart shapes into the dough.
Stuff hand pies with different fruits such as cherries, bananas, apples, and more.

Air Fryer Donuts

Servings: 8
Cooking Time: 7 Minutes

Ingredients:
- 1 3/4 cup self rising flour
- 1 cup vanilla yogurt
- For the glaze
- 1 1/2 cups powdered sugar sifted
- 1-2 tablespoons water or milk
- 2 tablespoons rainbow sprinkles optional

Directions:

1. In a large mixing bowl, add your flour and yogurt and mix well, until a thick dough remains. If the dough is too thin, add more flour. If the dough is too thick, add more yogurt.
2. Lightly flour a kitchen surface and transfer the dough onto it. Knead it several times until smooth. Divide the dough into 8 equal portions. Roll out each portion of dough into a long, sausage shape and connect both sides to form a donut.
3. Line an air fryer basket with parchment paper. Place 2-4 donuts on them (depending on how big your air fryer is), ensuring the donuts are at least half an inch apart, to ensure they have room to rise and spread.
4. Air fry the donuts at 200C/400F for 7-8 minutes, or until firm on the outside. Repeat the process until all the donuts are cooked.
5. Let the donuts cool completely. While cooling, prepare the glaze. Sift the powdered sugar into a large bowl. Add 1-2 tablespoons of water (or milk) and mix until a thick and smooth glaze remains.
6. Dip each donut in the glaze and place them on a wire rack. If desired, top with sprinkles.

Notes
TO STORE: Leftover donuts can be stored in the refrigerator, covered, for up to five days.
TO FREEZE: Place the donuts in an airtight container and store them in the freezer for up to six months.

Apple Pie In The Air Fryer

Ingredients:
- 4 tablespoons butter
- 6 tablespoons brown sugar
- 1 teaspoon ground cinnamon
- 2 medium Granny Smith apples, diced
- 1 teaspoon cornstarch
- 2 teaspoons cold water
- ½ (14 ounce) package pastry for a 9-inch double crust pie

- cooking spray
- ½ tablespoon grape-seed oil
- ¼ cup powdered sugar
- 1 teaspoon milk, or more as needed

Directions:
1. Combine apples, butter, brown sugar, and cinnamon in a non-stick skillet. Cook over medium heat until apples have softened, about 5 minutes.
2. Dissolve cornstarch in cold water. Stir into apple mixture and cook until sauce thickens, about 1 minute. Remove apple pie filling from heat and set aside to cool while you prepare the crust.
3. Unroll pie crust on a lightly floured surface and roll out slightly to smooth the surface of the dough. Cut the dough into rectangles small enough so that 2 can fit in your air fryer at one time. Repeat with remaining crust until you have 8 equal rectangles, re-rolling some of the scraps of dough if needed.
4. Wet the outer edges of 4 rectangles with water and place some apple filling in the center about 1/2-inch from the edges. Roll out the remaining 4 rectangles so that they are slightly larger than the filled ones. Place these rectangles on top of the filling; crimp the edges with a fork to seal. Cut 4 small slits in the tops of the pies.
5. Brush the tops of 2 pies with grapeseed oil and transfer pies to into your air fryer.
6. Close your air fryer oven door and set the temperature to 385 degrees F (195 degrees C). Bake until golden brown, about 8 minutes. Remove pies from the basket and repeat with the remaining 2 pies.
7. Mix together powdered sugar and milk in a small bowl. Brush glaze on warm pies and allow to dry. Serve pies warm or at room temperature.
8. Enjoy!

Air Fryer Baked Apples
Servings: 2
Cooking Time: 15 Minutes

Ingredients:
- 2 Apples (I use Pink Lady)
- 1 tsp Butter, melted
- 1/2 tsp Cinnamon
- Topping Ingredients:
- 1/3 cup Old Fashioned / Rolled Oats
- 1 tbsp Butter, melted
- 1 tbsp Maple Syrup (or honey or rice malt syrup)
- 1 tsp Wholemeal / Whole Wheat Flour, (can sub for almond meal or all purpose flour / plain flour)
- 1/2 tsp Cinnamon

Directions:
1. Cut apples in half through the stem and use a knife or a spoon to remove the core, stem and seeds. Brush a tsp of butter evenly over the cut sides of the apples, then sprinkle over 1/2 tsp of cinnamon.
2. Mix topping ingredients together in a small bowl, then spoon on top of the apple halves evenly.
3. Place the apple halves carefully into the air fryer basket, then cook on 180C / 350F for 15 minutes or until softened.
4. Serve warm with ice cream or cream if desired.

Notes
TIPS FOR MAKING AIR FRYER BAKED APPLES
I love using Pink Lady apples when baking, but Granny Smith, Golden Delicious or Honeycrisp would all work well.
This recipe uses melted butter for brushing over the apples and in the topping. Melt your butter all at once (1 tbsp + 1 tsp) and use a bit to brush over the apple halves, then mix what's left with the rest of the topping ingredients.
I find 15 minutes is perfect for these baked apples but if you find the apples are still a bit firm cook for a few minutes longer.

You can cook these in the oven if you don't have an air fryer - 180C/ 350F for 20 minutes or until the apples are soft & the topping is browned.
If you have any baked apples leftover store in an airtight container for up to 2 days.

Air Fryer Doubletree Signature Cookie
Servings: 18
Cooking Time: 7 Minutes

Ingredients:
- 1 cup unsalted butter (two sticks)
- 3/4 cup sugar
- 3/4 cup brown sugar
- 2 large eggs
- 1 1/4 teaspoon vanilla
- 1/4 teaspoon lemon juice
- 2 1/4 cups all purpose flour
- 1/2 cup rolled oats
- 1 teaspoon baking soda
- 1 teaspoon salt
- 1 pinch cinnamon
- 2 2/3 cups semi-sweet chocolate chips
- 1 3/4 cups chopped walnuts

Directions:
1. In a large bowl, combine the butter, sugar, and brown sugar and beat together for about 1-2 minutes.
2. Add in the eggs, vanilla, and lemon juice. Continue mixing until the ingredients have combined, scraping the sides of the bowl if necessary.
3. Slowly add in the flour, oats, baking soda, salt, and cinnamon until a soft dough forms.
4. Stir in the chocolate chips and the walnuts, until they are well combined into the dough.
5. Using a small scoop, or medium spoon, drop dough into the air fryer basket, lined with parchment paper with small holes for venting.
6. Cook at 300 degrees Fahrenheit for 7 minutes, until the cookies are golden brown and no longer doughy on bottom.
7. Allow the cookies to cool for about a minute in the basket, so they can set enough to be lifted with a spatula.

NOTES
This recipe makes about 36 cookies, depending on how large you make them.

Air Fryer Biscuits
Servings: 8
Cooking Time: 10 Minutes

Ingredients:
- 1 can pillsbury biscuits
- 1 tablespoon butter

Directions:
1. Preheat air fryer to 330°F.
2. Place 4 biscuits into the air fryer basket and cook for 9-10 minutes, flipping halfway through cooking.
3. Repeat with remaining biscuits.
4. Serve with butter.

Air Fryer Ice Cream Cookie Sandwich

Ingredients:
- 1 1/3 c Flour
- 1/3 c Coconut Sugar
- 1/4 c Brown Sugar
- 1 1/2 sticks of Butter
- 4 tbsp Honey
- 3 tbsp Whole Milk
- 1 tbsp Cocoa Powder
- 1 tsp Vanilla Essence
- 1c Chocolate Chips

Directions:
1. Add Butter and Sugars into a large mixing bowl - using an electric beater, mix the Sugar and Butter together thoroughly.
2. Next, Add Flour, Honey, Cocoa Powder, Vanilla, and Milk - Mix well!
3. To get the best results, use your hands! coat in flour and combine.
4. Add the Chocolate Chips a bit at a time.
5. Make about 12- 17 balls of cookie dough

6. Place some Parchment paper into your Air Fryer to prevent the cookies from sticking.
7. Arrange cookies about 2 inches apart.
8. Cook for 15 minutes at 350°
9. Bonus Round!
10. In your Blender add 1 cup of Heavy Whipping Cream, 1 cup of Half and Half,1/4 cup Sugar, 1 whole Vanilla Bean, 1/2 tsp of Salt, and 4 cups of Ice.
11. Blend until mixture becomes, Ice Cream!
12. Enjoy!

Air-fryer Brownies

Servings: 9
Cooking Time: 45 Minutes

Ingredients:
- 1/3 cup butter, cubed
- 1-1/2 cups 60% cacao bittersweet chocolate baking chips, divided
- 2 large eggs, room temperature
- 3/4 cup sugar
- 2 tablespoons water
- 1 teaspoon vanilla extract
- 3/4 cup all-purpose flour
- 1/4 teaspoon baking soda
- 1/4 teaspoon salt

Directions:
1. Preheat air fryer to 325°. Line a 6-in. square or round cake pan with parchment, letting ends extend up sides. In a small microwave-safe bowl, melt butter and 1 cup chocolate chips; stir until smooth. Cool slightly. In a small bowl, beat sugar and eggs. Stir in water and vanilla. Combine flour, baking soda and salt; gradually add to chocolate mixture. Fold in remaining 1/2 cup chocolate chips.
2. Pour into prepared pan. Bake until a toothpick inserted in center comes out with moist crumbs, 40-45 minutes (do not overbake). Tent with foil as needed to prevent overbrowning. Cool on a wire rack.
3. Lifting with parchment, remove brownies from pan. Cut into squares.

Grammy's Jam Thumbprints

Ingredients:
- 2/3 cup butter
- 1/3 cup sugar
- 2 eggs (yolks separated; whites saved)
- 1 tsp vanilla
- ½ tsp salt
- 1 ½ cup flour
- Walnuts, chopped
- Strawberry preserves

Directions:
1. Cream butter and sugar until fluffy
2. Add in yolks, vanilla, and salt – beat well.
3. Gradually add in flour.
4. Shape into ¾ inch balls. Dip into beaten egg whites. Then roll in finely chopped walnuts.
5. Place on greased cookies sheet. Press down in center with thumb.
6. Bake in your Air Fryer Oven at 350*F for 10-12 minutes. Let cool.
7. Add strawberry preserves into the thumbprint.

Air Fryer Frozen Turnover Pastries

Servings: 2
Cooking Time: 16 Minutes

Ingredients:
- 2 Frozen Turnover Pastries
- whipped cream ,optional

Directions:
1. Place the frozen pastries in the air fryer basket and spread in an even layer (make sure they aren't overlapping). No oil spray is needed.
2. Air Fry at 360°F/180°C for 8 minutes. Flip the pastries over.
3. Continue to Air Fry at 360°F/180°C for another 6-8 minutes or until to your preferred doneness. Serve with whipped cream if desired.

NOTES
No Oil Necessary. Cook Frozen - Do not thaw first.
Cook in a single layer in the air fryer basket.

Recipe timing is based on a non-preheated air fryer. If cooking in multiple batches back to back, the following batches may cook a little quicker.

Recipes were tested in 3.7 to 6 qt. air fryers. If using a larger air fryer, they might cook quicker so adjust cooking time.

Air Fryer Celebration Bites

Servings: 24
Cooking Time: 10 Minutes

Ingredients:
- 4 sheets frozen shortcrust pastry, partially thawed
- 1 egg, lightly beaten
- 24 Mars Celebrations chocolates, unwrapped
- Cinnamon sugar, for dusting
- Icing sugar, for dusting
- Whipped cream, to serve
- Select all Ingredients:

Directions:
1. Cut each sheet of pastry into 6 rectangles. Brush lightly with egg. Place 1 chocolate in the centre of each piece of pastry. Fold over pastry to enclose chocolate. Trim pastry, pressing edges to seal. Place on a baking paper-lined tray. Brush tops with a little egg. Sprinkle liberally with cinnamon sugar.
2. Place a sheet of baking paper in the air-fryer basket, making sure paper is 1cm smaller than the basket to allow air to circulate. Place 6 pockets in the basket, being careful not to overlap. Cook on 190°C for 8-9 minutes or until golden and pastry is cooked through. Transfer to a plate. Repeat with remaining pockets.
3. Dust with icing sugar. Serve warm with whipped cream.

Air Fried Oreos

Servings: 8
Cooking Time: 5 Minutes

Ingredients:
- 8 Oreos
- 1 Pillsbury crescents (8 count)
- 3 Tbsp powdered sugar optional

Directions:
1. Preheat the Air Fryer to 325 degrees Fahrenheit.
2. Remove the crescent rolls from the can and lay them out on a flat surface.
3. Carefully wrap one Oreo into each crescent roll sheet.
4. Once the air fryer is ready, prepare the basket with oil or with a sheet or parchment paper.
5. Add the wrapped Oreos onto the air fryer basket in a single layer, keep room in between for them to cook.
6. Cook on 325 degrees Fahrenheit for 5-6 minutes, or the tops have turned until golden brown.
7. Allow the fried Oreos to cool for a minute before removing them from the basket.
8. Sprinkle the fried Oreos with a little powdered sugar and serve immediately.

NOTES

Save this snack idea for when you're craving something sweet and you need it fast! It's a crowd-pleaser.

Use different flavored Oreos such as vanilla, chocolate, mint, and definitely go for the Double stuff.

Leek & Mushroom Pie

Ingredients:
- 300g/2 leeks
- 500g mushrooms
- 3 Cloves garlic
- 1 Tbsp corn flour
- 125ml vegetable stock
- 2 Tbsp Dijon
- 250ml oatly cream

- 5g fresh thyme
- Vegan milk, for brushing the pastry
- 1 roll frozen puff pastry, defrosted (vegan friendly)

Directions:
1. Thinly slice the leeks and mushrooms. Using sauté on your Instant Pot or a frying pan, cook the leeks until just starting to soften, then add the mushrooms. Cook until the mushrooms are soft and browned. Add the garlic and cook for 1 more minute.
2. Mix the corn flour with a little vegetable stock to form a smooth slurry, then pour the corn flour mixture, remaining tock and oatly cream into the sautéed vegetables and cook until thickened. Pick the thyme from the woody stems and add this to the pie filling. Mix in the Dijon, and season to taste with salt and pepper.
3. Spoon the filling into a suitable size dish to fit in your Instant Vortex. An 18cm pie dish is perfect and allows plenty of room for the air to circulate and ensure the pie cooks evenly. Unroll your defrosted pastry, then cut a circle big enough to cover your pie. Place your pastry circle on top of your filling and crimp the edges to the pie dish to seal everything together. Poke a few small holes in the centre of the pie to allow the steam to escape, then brush the pastry with a little oat milk,
4. Place the pie into the basket of your air fryer. Select Air Fry, set the time to 25 minutes and the temperature to 170°C. Cook the pie until the pastry is beautifully puffed and crisp. Once cooked, remove the pie from the Vortex and serve immediately alongside your sides of choice.

Air Fryer Grilled Cheese
Servings: 2
Cooking Time: 8 Minutes

Ingredients:
- 4 slices bread white, whole wheat, or gluten free
- 1 tablespoon mayonnaise
- 1 tablespoon butter
- 1/2 cup mozzarella cheese shredded
- 1/2 cup cheddar cheese

Directions:
1. Spread mayonnaise on one side of each slice of bread. Next, add half a tablespoon of butter on top of the mayonnaise. This is for the outside of the grilled cheese.
2. On one side of two pieces of bread the non-mayonnaise/butter side, add half the mozzarella cheese and half the cheddar cheese on each piece of bread. Place the second piece of bread on each one, mayonnaise/butter side on the outside.
3. Preheat the air fryer to 200C/400F.
4. Generously spray the air fryer basket and place one sandwich in it. Add two toothpicks to prevent the bread from sticking.
5. Air fry for 8-9 minutes, flipping halfway through. Once the exterior is golden, remove it from the air fryer. Repeat the process with the second one.
6. Slice the sandwiches in half and enjoy.

Notes
TO STORE: Place leftovers in an airtight container and store them in the refrigerator for up to 3 days.
TO REHEAT: Reheat the refrigerated grilled cheese in the air fryer or a non-stick skillet.

Roast Dinner Yorkshire Pudding Wraps

Ingredients:
- 1 x 20cm/8" cake tin
- 90g flour
- 1 pinch salt
- 20ml water
- 2 eggs
- 80ml full fat milk
- 2g fresh chives, thinly sliced
- Oil for the tin
- Serving Suggestions:
- Roast beef, horseradish, roast potatoes (reheated until crisp), leftover green veg (we used Brussel sprouts, and sautéed greens). Add mustard if desired.
- Sautéed mushrooms or nut roast, Vortex crispy chickpeas (lightly oiled, Air Fry on 205°C for 6 mins), roast potatoes, roasted butternut, sauce of choice (a plant based white sauce, or salsa verde is lovely here!)
- Roast Chicken, stuffing, gravy, cauliflower cheese, honey roasted carrots broccoli – All reheated in the Vortex Air Fryer (Grill on 205°C for 4 mins)
- Roast Lamb, Mint sauce, minted peas, mixed roasted veggies, rosemary roast potatoes
- No Roast leftovers? No problem!
- Cook some sausages and serve with mustard mayo (1Tbso Dijon +2 Tbsp Mayo) and buttery sautéed cabbage

Directions:
1. Add the flour and salt in a bowl and make a well in the middle. Add the water, eggs and milk and whisk the batter until no lumps remain. Then mix in the chives. Place the batter into the fridge to rest for as long as you can. Resting the batter is an important step as this will yield ever loftier results the longer the batter sits. 30 minutes before you are ready to cook, remove the batter from the fridge and allow it to come back to room temperature. Gather your roast dinner fillings, and reheat them as needed in the air fryer then set aside to keep warm while you cook the York shire pudding wraps.
2. Drizzle your sponge tin with oil until it covers the base of the tin in a 1mm layer. Place the oiled tin into the basket of the Instant Vortex Air Fryer. Select Air Fry, set the temperature to 205°C and the time to 8 minutes. Press Start and allow the air fryer to preheat with the cake tin inside. When prompted, open the drawer and pour exactly half of your batter into the heated cake tin.
3. Cook the Yorkshire pudding until deeply golden and puffy (ignore when prompted to turn food.) Once cooked remove the hot Yorkshire pudding wrap from the cake tin with tongs, then set aside to keep warm. Add in a little more oil into the cake tin, then repeat the cooking process with the remaining batter.
4. Once both pudding wraps are cooked, load them up with your favourite leftovers, roll up and serve immediately.
5. Tips for the puffiest pudding:
6. Rest time: The single most important step. Resting the batter will increase the rise of the puddings, and lead to a tastier and more complex final flavour. Aim for a few hours minimum if you can, or let them sit for up to three days for gravity defying pudding. Warm vs cold batter: A personal choice. Room temperature batter will yield tall, crispy puddings with a hollow core. Cold batter will create denser puddings with a pronounced cup.
7. Preheat your cake tin and oil for a great puff.

How To Cook Patty Pan Squash

Servings: 6
Cooking Time: 10 Minutes

Ingredients:
- BASIC PATTY PAN SQUASH:
- 2 lb Patty pan squash (cut into pieces of the same size; you can cut them in half, or into quarters or wedges if they are larger)

- 2 tbsp Olive oil
- 1 tsp Sea salt
- 1/2 tsp Black pepper
- OPTIONAL FLAVOR BOOSTERS:
- 2 tsp Italian seasoning
- 1 tsp Garlic powder
- 1/2 tsp Crushed red pepper flakes

Directions:
1. SAUTEED PATTYPAN SQUASH:
2. Heat the olive oil in a large skillet over medium-high heat.
3. Add the pattypans and arrange, cut side down, in a single layer. Season with salt, pepper, and any flavor boosters, if using. (Work in batches if they don't fit in a single layer.)
4. Sear the squash for 3-5 minutes, without moving, until golden on the bottom. Flip and repeat until golden on the other side.
5. ROASTED PATTYPAN SQUASH:
6. Preheat the oven to 450 degrees F (232 degrees C).
7. In a large bowl, toss the pattypan squash with olive oil, salt, pepper, and any flavor boosters, if using.
8. Transfer the squash to a baking sheet and arrange, cut side down, in a single layer.
9. Roast pattypan squash for 15-20 minutes until tender and golden brown on the bottom. (If desired, you can stir halfway through for more even browning.)
10. GRILLED PATTYPAN SQUASH:
11. Preheat the outdoor grill for at least 10 minutes, or a grill pan on the stovetop, over medium-high heat.
12. In a large bowl, toss the pattypan squash with olive oil, salt, pepper, and any flavor boosters, if using. (If using an outdoor grill, larger squash pieces work best, so they won't fall through the grates.)
13. Place the squash, cut side down, onto the grill or grill pan in a single layer.
14. Grill for 3-4 minutes, until the grill marks form on the bottom. Flip and grill for 3-4 more minutes on the other side, until the squash is tender.
15. AIR FRYER PATTYPAN SQUASH:
16. In a large bowl, toss the pattypan squash with olive oil, salt, pepper, and any flavor boosters, if using.
17. Place the pattypan squash in the air fryer basket, cut side down, in a single layer. (Cook in batches if they don't all fit in a single layer.)
18. Air fry for 10-12 minutes at 400 degrees F (204 degrees C), until crispy and golden.

Air Fryer Molten Lava Cakes

Ingredients:
- 110g butter
- 200g chocolate
- 2 large eggs
- 2 egg yolks
- 75g sugar
- 1 tsp vanilla essence
- 1/4 cup flour

Directions:
1. Grease 6 ramekins and dust with cocoa powder. Leave aside.
2. In a bowl melt the butter and chocolate in a bowl until the chocolate is melted (20 second intervals). Mix together until combined. When the mixture has cooled down slightly add in the eggs, mix, and then add in the egg yokes. Mix until combined and add in the flour, sugar and vanilla. Once the batter is smooth pour into the ramekins about half way.
3. Heat the air fryer to 200 degrees Celsius for 8 minutes. Once heated add in the ramekins. After 8 minutes check the cakes and if you like them runny remove with a thick cloth. You can bake further to 9-10 minutes as well. Once you remove from the air fryer the cakes need to be removed from the ramekins as soon as possible or they will continue to cook. Loosen the sides with a knife and gently tilt them out.
4. Serve immediately with ice cream, fresh cream or just as is. Enjoy

POULTRY RECIPES

Italian Chicken Skewers

Ingredients:
- 1 lb. skinless and boneless chicken breasts, cut into large cubes
- salt and pepper to taste
- 2 tbsp tomato paste
- ¼ cup olive oil, plus more for drizzling
- 3 garlic cloves, minced
- 1 tbsp fresh Italian parsley, chopped
- 1 French baguette, cut into cubes

Directions:
1. Season chicken with salt and pepper to taste.
2. In a medium sized bowl, combine the tomato paste, olive oil, garlic cloves and chopped parsley to make the marinade. Add the chicken and marinade to a Ziploc bag and toss to fully coat. Refrigerate for 30 minutes.
3. Skewer your chicken and bread. Drizzle with olive oil and season with salt and pepper. Using your Air Fryer Oven, place your skewers in the appliance and use the rotisserie setting. Air fry the skewers at 400°F for 10 minutes.
4. Garnish with parmesan and parsley and enjoy!

Air Fryer Frozen Chicken Pot Pie

Servings: 2
Cooking Time: 24 Minutes

Ingredients:
- 2 frozen chicken pot pies
- salt and pepper to taste

Directions:
1. Preheat the air fryer to 360°F.
2. Place the chicken pot pies in the air fryer basket.
3. Cook for 20-24 minutes or until the crust is golden brown and the filling is warm.
4. Season as desired.

Air Fryer Southern Fried Chicken

Servings: 4
Cooking Time: 32 Minutes

Ingredients:
- 2½ pounds chicken, cut into pieces
- House Seasoning, to taste
- 3 large eggs
- 1 cupHot Sauce
- 2 cups self-rising flour
- oil, for spraying

Directions:
1. Season chicken well with House Seasoning. In a medium bowl, beat together eggs and The Lady & Sons Signature Hot Sauce. Place flour in a shallow dish. Dip chicken pieces in egg mixture, then dredge in flour. Place on a baking sheet lined with parchment paper.
2. Working in batches of 4, spray tops of chicken with oil and place in air fryer basket. Spray chicken again. Set temperature to 350°F, and air fry for 15 minutes. Turn chicken, spray with oil, and air fry for 10 minutes more. Turn chicken, spray with oil, and air fry for 10 minutes more. Turn chicken again, and spray with oil. Increase temperature to 400°F, and air fry for 7 minutes. After chicken has reached an internal temperature of 165°F, remove to a serving platter and cover to keep warm. Repeat with remaining chicken.

Air Fryer Chicken Wings

Servings: 4
Cooking Time: 35 Minutes

Ingredients:
- 2 lb Chicken wings (flats and drumettes, either fresh or thawed from frozen)
- 1 tbsp Olive oil (optional)
- 2 tsp Baking powder
- 3/4 tsp Sea salt

- 1/4 tsp Black pepper

Directions:
1. Pat the chicken wings very dry with paper towels. (This will help them get crispy.)
2. In a large bowl, toss the wings with baking powder, olive oil (if using), sea salt and black pepper.
3. Place the chicken wings in the air fryer in a single layer, without touching too much. (Cook in batches if they don't fit.)
4. Air fry the chicken wings for 15 minutes at 250 degrees F. (If your wings are frozen, add an extra 10 minutes at this step.)
5. Flip the wings over. Increase the air fryer temperature to 430 degrees F (or the highest your air fryer goes). Air fry for about 15 to 20 minutes, until chicken wings are done and crispy.

Air Fryer Bone In Chicken Thighs

Servings: 3
Cooking Time: 20 Minutes

Ingredients:
- 3 bone in, skin on chicken thighs
- Salt and pepper, to taste
- 2 teaspoons olive oil
- ½ teaspoon garlic powder
- ½ teaspoon onion powder
- 1 tablespoon poultry seasoning

Directions:
1. Preheat your air fryer to 380 degrees F.
2. Season your chicken thighs with salt and pepper. Drizzle the olive oil over the thighs. Combine the garlic powder, onion powder, and poultry seasoning in a small bowl. Rub the seasoning onto your thighs till they are covered. You may have some remaining seasoning.
3. Place your chicken thighs in the air fryer basket and cook for 12 minutes, and then flip them. Continue to cook for an additional 6 to 7 minutes or until a meat thermometer reads an internal temperature of 165 degrees F.
4. Allow them to rest for a few minutes and serve.
5. Optional: Garnish them with fresh parsley.

NOTES
HOW TO REHEAT AIR FRYER BONE IN CHICKEN THIGHS
Preheat your air fryer to 350 degrees F.
Place chicken thighs in the air fryer basket and cook for 5 minutes, or till heated through.

Air Fryer Yogurt Marinated Chicken

Servings: 4
Cooking Time: 16 Minutes

Ingredients:
- 4 boneless, skinless chicken breasts
- 1 cup yogurt plain or Greek
- 1/2 tsp parsley flakes
- 1/2 tsp garlic powder
- 1/2 tsp paprika
- ½ tsp kosher salt
- ¼ tsp black pepper

Directions:
1. In a large sealable bag, or medium bowl, combine the yogurt with the parsley flakes, garlic powder, paprika, salt, and black pepper. Add chicken and toss together to coat chicken. Seal bag or cover bowl with plastic wrap, and refrigerate for 4-6 hours.
2. Remove from the bag and place the pieces of chicken in a single layer in a lightly sprayed air fryer basket.
3. Air Fry at 380 degrees F for 8-10 minutes on each side.
4. Cook until golden brown, and the chicken has an internal temperature of 165 degrees F.

NOTES
Variations
Add different seasonings - You can change the seasonings easily by adding onion powder, cayenne pepper, fresh ginger, garam masala, lemon zest, garlic cloves, or anything else that you want to add.

Make chicken kabobs - If you want to really have fun with this recipe, get some wooden skewers and make kabobs! The quick marinade is perfect for marinating the chicken, and you can then add the pieces to the skewers to cook over the open fire or outdoor grill.

Air Fryer Turkey Meatloaf
Servings: 2-4

Ingredients:
- 2 tsp. extra-virgin olive oil
- 1 small yellow onion, finely chopped
- 3 cloves garlic, minced
- 1/2 tsp. finely chopped rosemary
- 1 lb. ground turkey (preferably dark meat)
- 1/3 c. fine bread crumbs
- 1/4 c. chopped fresh parsley leaves
- 1 large egg, beaten to blend
- 2 tsp. Worcestershire sauce
- 1 tsp. Dijon mustard
- 1/2 tsp. kosher salt
- 1/4 tsp. freshly ground black pepper
- Olive oil cooking spray
- 1/4 c. ketchup
- 1 tbsp. light brown sugar

Directions:
1. In a medium nonstick skillet over medium-high heat, heat oil. Cook onion, stirring, until soft and golden, about 4 minutes. Add garlic and rosemary; cook, stirring, until fragrant, about 1 minute.
2. Scrape onion mixture into a medium bowl and let cool slightly. Add ground turkey, bread crumbs, parsley, egg, Worcestershire, mustard, salt, and pepper and mix with your hands to combine. Divide turkey mixture in half. Form into 2 (5"-by-2 1/2") loaves.
3. Lightly coat an air-fryer basket with cooking spray. Place turkey loaves in basket. Cook at 350°, flipping halfway through, until an instant-read thermometer inserted into center registers 165°, about 30 minutes.
4. In a small bowl, combine ketchup and brown sugar. Flip meatloaves and spoon glaze over top. Continue to cook at 350° until glaze is set, about 2 minutes more.

Air Fryer Asian-glazed Boneless Chicken Thighs
Servings: 4
Cooking Time: 30 Minutes

Ingredients:
- 8 boneless, skinless chicken thighs, fat trimmed (32 oz total)
- 1/4 cup low sodium soy sauce
- 2 1/2 tablespoons balsamic vinegar
- 1 tablespoon honey
- 3 cloves garlic (crushed)
- 1 teaspoon Sriracha hot sauce
- 1 teaspoon fresh grated ginger
- 1 scallion (green only sliced for garnish)

Directions:
1. In a small bowl combine the balsamic, soy sauce, honey, garlic, sriracha and ginger and mix well.
2. Pour half of the marinade (1/4 cup) into a large bowl with the chicken, covering all the meat and marinate at least 2 hours, or as long as overnight.
3. Reserve the remaining sauce for later.
4. Preheat the air fryer to 400F.
5. Remove the chicken from the marinade and transfer to the air fryer basket.
6. Cook in batches 14 minutes, turning halfway until cooked through in the center.
7. Meanwhile, place the remaining sauce in a small pot and cook over medium-low heat until it reduces slightly and thickens, about 1 to 2 minutes.
8. To serve, drizzle the sauce over the chicken and top with scallions.

Air-fryer Buffalo Wings

Servings: 4

Ingredients:
- 1 ½ teaspoons paprika
- ½ teaspoon garlic powder
- ½ teaspoon onion powder
- ½ teaspoon ground pepper
- 3 ½ to 4 pounds chicken wings, separated if necessary
- ½ cup Buffalo-style hot sauce (such as Frank's RedHot)
- 2 tablespoons unsalted butter
- ¼ cup ranch dressing
- 2 carrots, cut into sticks
- 1 stalk celery, cut into sticks

Directions:
1. Preheat oven to 200 degrees F. Preheat air fryer to 375 degrees F. Combine paprika, garlic powder, onion powder and pepper in a large bowl. Add wings and toss to coat. Let stand for 10 minutes.
2. Add half of the wings to the air-fryer basket; cook for 15 minutes. Turn the wings; continue to cook until they're crispy and a thermometer inserted in the thickest portion registers 165 degrees F, about 5 minutes. Arrange the wings in a single layer on a baking sheet; transfer to the oven to keep warm. Repeat the process with the remaining wings.
3. Cook hot sauce and butter in a small saucepan over medium-high heat, whisking often, until the butter melts and the mixture is smooth, 2 to 3 minutes.
4. Transfer the wings to a large bowl. Add the butter sauce and toss to coat. Serve alongside ranch dressing, carrots and celery.

Bbq Chicken Wings

Ingredients:
- 3 cm piece of fresh ginger, peeled and grated
- 1 garlic clove, crushed
- 3 tbsp orange marmalade
- 2 tbsp clear honey
- 1 tbsp sesame oil
- 2 tsp soy sauce
- 1 ½ tsp Chinese five-spice
- ½ tsp grated orange zest

Directions:
1. Mix all of the ingredients, except for the chicken wings, in a large bowl.
2. Dip the chicken wings into the mixture, cover and refrigerate for at least 2 hours or overnight, turning occasionally.
3. Plug in and switch on the air fryer at the mains power supply.
4. Set the temperature to 200ºC and the time to approx. 15 mins and carefully place the chicken wings into the relevant cooking compartment.
5. Check that the chicken wings are cooked through before serving.
6. Serve immediately with your choice of sides.

Air Fryer Chicken Strips

Ingredients:
- 1¼ lbs. chicken breast tenders
- 2 eggs, whisked
- 1 1/4 cup almond flour
- 2 Tbsp. coconut flour
- 1½ tsp. garlic powder
- 1½ tsp. onion powder
- 1/2 tsp. sea salt
- 1/2 tsp. black pepper
- 1/2 tsp. cayenne
- 1/3 cup buffalo sauce

Directions:
1. In a shallow dish, whisk the eggs.
2. In another shallow dish, combine the flours, garlic, onion, salt, pepper, and cayenne.
3. With a paper towel, pat the chicken breast tenders dry and place on a plate.
4. Dunk the chicken tenders into the egg wash, letting excess egg drip off before coating the chicken tender generously with breading. For a thicker breading, repeat the egg wash and breading step once more.

5. Air fry at 400 for 8 minutes. Flip and then air fry 8 additional minutes.
6. Allow to sit for 3-4 minutes before brushing with buffalo sauce. Enjoy!

Air Fryer Chicken Cordon Bleu
Servings: 2
Cooking Time: 25 Minutes
Ingredients:
- 2 small boneless, skinless chicken breasts
- 4 slices swiss cheese
- 4 slices ham
- 3 tablespoons mayonnaise
- 2 tablespoons Dijon mustard
- Kosher salt, to taste
- Black pepper, to taste
- 1 cup panko breadcrumbs
- DIJON SAUCE
- 1 tablespoon unsalted butter
- 1 tablespoon flour
- ⅔ cup milk
- 1 tablespoon Dijon mustard
- 2 tablespoons grated Parmesan cheese
- Kosher salt and black pepper, to taste
- Fresh parsley, for garnish

Directions:
1. Cut a pocket into each chicken breast. Place a cheese slice on top of a slice of ham, then another slice of ham and cheese. Roll them up so the cheese is inside. Place the rolls inside each pocket and close them with 2 toothpicks if necessary.
2. In a small bowl, mix the mayonnaise, mustard, and a dash of salt and pepper together. Spread it in a thin layer all over the chicken.
3. Place the breadcrumbs on a large, shallow plate. Carefully roll the chicken in the breadcrumbs until fully coated.
4. Preheat the air fryer to 370 degrees F then place the chicken in a single layer inside. Spray the top of the chicken with cooking oil spray.
5. Air fry for 20-25 minutes, or until the internal temperature reaches 165 degrees F.
6. While the chicken is cooking, make the sauce: melt the butter in a small saucepan set over medium heat. Whisk in flour and cook for 1 minute.
7. Slowly whisk in the milk and whisk until the mixture is blended and smooth.
8. Add the mustard and Parmesan and simmer for 2-3 minutes, whisking constantly, until thickened. Season with salt and pepper to taste. Serve over chicken.

Kfc Nashville Hot Chicken Tenders
Ingredients:
- 1 lb chicken tenders
- ¾ cup milk
- 2 Tbsp hot sauce
- ¾ cup panko bread crumbs
- 1 tsp paprika
- ½ tsp Italian seasoning
- ½ tsp salt
- ½ garlic powder
- ½ onion powder
- ¼ tsp black pepper
- Salt and pepper to taste
- Nonstick cooking spray
- Hot Paste
- ½ cup peanut oil
- 2 Tbsp brown sugar
- 1 ½ Tbsp cayenne pepper
- 1 tsp paprika
- 1 tsp dry mustard
- 1 tsp garlic powder
- 1 tsp salt

Directions:
1. Create a dredging station by whisking milk and hot sauce in one bowl. In a separate bowl, mix panko bread crumbs, paprika, Italian seasoning, salt, garlic powder, onion powder, and black pepper.
2. Season tenders with a little salt and pepper. Start by coating chicken tenders with milk mixture and drain off excess milk, then coat chicken in panko bread crumbs mixture, ensuring all of the chicken is coated.

3. Place chicken in greased air fryer basket or use a parchment sheet liner. Cook on 370 degrees for 16 minutes, flipping and spraying chicken halfway through cooking, until chicken is fully cooked and has reached a temperature of at least 165 degrees Fahrenheit.
4. Meanwhile, when there are about 5 minutes left on the chicken, create the hot paste.
5. Combine the brown sugar, cayenne pepper, paprika, dry mustard, garlic powder, and salt to a large bowl.
6. Warm up your peanut oil in a medium-sized saucepan over medium heat. Once your oil starts to bubble and simmer, pour it over your spice mixture and whisk to combine.
7. Once chicken tenders are done, remove from air fryer and add them to the hot paste and toss, making sure the hot paste covers all of the chicken. Serve with pickle slices and enjoy!

Air Fryer Buffalo Chicken Egg Rolls
Servings: 8-10
Cooking Time: 8 Minutes

Ingredients:
- 3 cups shredded chicken
- 2 tablespoons Cavender's Greek seasoning
- 1/2 cup buffalo sauce
- 1 cup cheddar cheese, shredded
- 1/2 cup greek yogurt
- 8-10 egg roll wrappers

Directions:
1. Preheat your air fryer 350 degrees.
2. Mix the shredded chicken, greek seasoning, buffalo sauce, cheddar cheese, and greek yogurt in a large bowl.
3. Place two heaping tablespoons of mixture onto the center of an egg roll wrapper.
4. Wet the edges of the wrapper and fold it close. Fold the left and right corners in overlapping one another.
5. Fold the bottom corner up to begin to close the egg roll.
6. Fold and roll the top corner down enclosing the egg roll.
7. Cook for 5 minutes on one side and 3 on the next. make sure you spray each side with the EVO Oil Sprayer.
8. Remove and let cool before eating.
9. Dip in your favorite dressing, I recommend blue cheese or ranch.

Crispy Air Fryer Chicken Thighs
Servings: 4
Cooking Time: 20 Minutes

Ingredients:
- 2 lb. bone-in chicken thighs (we used 4)
- 1/2 tablespoon garlic powder
- 2 teaspoons paprika
- 1 tablespoon dried thyme
- ½ teaspoon salt
- 2 teaspoons brown sugar
- 2 tablespoons olive oil

Directions:
1. Preheat the air fryer to 400°F and spray the inside of the basket with non-stick cooking spray.
2. Add the garlic powder, paprika, dried thyme, salt, and brown sugar to a bowl and mix until combined.
3. Pat the chicken thighs dry with a piece of paper towel and sprinkle the dry rub over the chicken thighs. Be sure the dry rub covers the entire chicken thigh.
4. Place the chicken thighs skin side down into the air fryer and drizzle the chicken thighs with olive oil. You may have to do this in two batches depending on the size of your air fryer.
5. Set the air fryer for 8 minutes, flip the chicken thighs, and cook the chicken thighs for an additional 6-10 minutes depending on the size of your thighs.
6. If the internal temperature of the chicken is 165°F and the skin is crispy, remove the chicken thighs from the air fryer. If you would like your chicken thighs crispier,

cook them for an additional 2 minutes. Let the chicken sit for 3-5 minutes and enjoy.

Air Fryer Chicken Kabobs
Servings: 6
Cooking Time: 10 Minutes

Ingredients:
- 1 lb boneless skinless chicken breast cut into bite sizes pieces about 2 chicken breasts
- 1/3 cup sweet chili sauce
- ½ tbsp Herbs de Provence
- 1 tsp smoked paprika
- ½ tsp red pepper flakes
- 2 tbsp vegetable oil
- 1 tsp garlic granules
- Salt and black pepper to taste
- 3 Bell peppers cut into big chunks
- 1 Zucchini chopped into big chunks
- 1 large Onion chopped into big chunks i used red onion

Directions:
1. To a large mixing bowl, combine chicken pieces, salt, black pepper, red pepper flakes and mix to combine.
2. Add chopped bell peppers, chopped zucchini, onions, smoked paprika, herb de Provence, sweet chilli sauce, vegetable oil and mix all to combine.
3. Cover the bowl with a plastic wrap/cling film and marinate for at least 30 minutes or longer if time is not of the essence.
4. When you are ready to cook, thread the marinated chicken and vegetables on the skewer, repeat the process until all is exhausted.
5. Preheat the air fryer at 200C/400F for 5 minutes then spray the air fryer basket with cooking oil
6. Arrange the chicken skewers in the air fryer basket in a single layer making sure it is not overcrowded (you may have to cook the chicken in batches).
7. Cook at 400F/200C for 10 minutes or until fully cooked and the chicken is no longer white when cut into. carefully flipping the kabob halfway through.
8. PS: The internal temperature of cooked chicken should read 165F/73C when checked with an instant read or meat thermometer.

NOTES
Hot grill or griddle pan Directions:
Tread the marinated cubed chicken and vegetables into a skewer and cook on a hot grill or griddle pan flipping every 2 to 3 minutes until cooked through.
Tips
If you want a grill mark on your chicken skewers then place an air fryer rack/trivet inside the air fryer basket before cooking.
Cut the chicken and vegetables into even sizes so they cook evenly

Butter-herb Roasted Whole Chicken

Ingredients:
- 1/2 cup butter, softened
- 2 teaspoons fresh thyme leaves, chopped
- 2 teaspoons fresh sage leaves, chopped
- 2 cloves garlic, minced
- 1 1/4 teaspoons salt
- 1 teaspoon pepper
- 1 whole chicken (about 4 lb)
- 3 large carrots, cut into 1-inch pieces
- 1 lb fingerling potatoes
- 1 onion, cut into wedges
- 2 Tablespoons olive oil

Directions:
1. In small bowl, mix butter, chopped thyme, sage, garlic, 3/4 teaspoon of the salt and 1/2 teaspoon of the pepper.
2. To truss the chicken: Place chicken breast side up. Tuck the wings under the breast as best you can to not burn the wing tips. Using kitchen twine, start the string at the top of the breasts, overtop of the legs, back under the legs and pulling them together to tie a simple knot. This ensures that the chicken will cook evenly.

3. Rub mixture under and on skin of chicken.
4. In large bowl, toss carrots, potatoes and onions with oil and remaining 1/2 teaspoon salt and 1/2 teaspoon pepper.
5. Remove the crisper tray from the Steam Air Fryer basket and dump in the seasoned vegetables. Place the whole chicken on top.
6. Cook at 360°F for 55 minutes -1 hour or until thermometer reads at least 165°F.

Jerk Chicken Wings

Ingredients:
- 1 kg chicken wings
- 75 g plain flour
- 1 egg, beaten
- 2 tbsp sugar
- 1 tbsp ground allspice
- 1 tbsp ground black pepper
- 4 ½ tsp onion powder
- 4 ½ tsp dried thyme, crushed
- 1 ½ - 3 tsp ground red pepper
- 1 ½ tsp salt
- ¾ tsp ground nutmeg
- ¼ tsp garlic powder
- Cooking spray

Directions:
1. Mix all of the ingredients, except for the chicken wings and cooking spray, in a large bowl to create your jerk seasoning.
2. Sprinkle the mixture onto the chicken wings and rub in.
3. Spray the chicken wings on all sides with cooking spray.
4. Plug in and switch on the air fryer at the mains power supply.
5. Set the temperature to 200°C and the time to approx. 30 mins and carefully place the chicken wings into the relevant cooking compartment.
6. Check that the chicken wings are cooked through before serving.
7. Serve immediately with your choice of sides.

Air Fryer Crispy Chicken Breasts

Servings: 4
Cooking Time: 16 Minutes

Ingredients:
- 4 chicken breasts about 5 oz each
- 2 eggs beaten
- ⅔ cup flour
- Bread Crumb Mixture
- ½ cup Panko bread crumbs
- ⅓ cup seasoned bread crumbs
- 1 teaspoons garlic powder
- 1 teaspoon Italian seasoning
- ½ teaspoon each salt and pepper
- cooking spray

Directions:
1. Preheat air fryer to 370°F.
2. Pound chicken breasts to an even thickness.
3. Beat eggs in a small bowl. Combine flour, salt and pepper in a shallow dish. In third dish, combine the bread crumb mixture.
4. Dredge the chicken with flour. Dip it into the egg and then into the bread crumbs.
5. Spray with cooking spray and place in a single layer in the air fryer basket.
6. Cook 16-19 minutes flipping the chicken over after 10 minutes.

Notes
Chicken should reach 165°F.

Chicken Shawarma Flatbreads

Servings: 4
Cooking Time: 30 Minutes

Ingredients:
- 1 3/4 cup The Pantry Self-Raising Flour
- 1 cup and 3 tablespoons Greek Style Natural Yoghurt
- 300g Chicken Thigh Fillets - diced
- 2 Red Onions
- 4 Garlic Cloves - finely chopped/grated
- Half pack Everyday Essentials Mozzarella
- 1 teaspoon of Cumin
- 1 teaspoon of Smoked Paprika
- 1 teaspoon of Cajun
- 1 teaspoon of Mixed Herbs

- Salt and Pepper
- Oil

Directions:
1. To make the flatbreads, add 1 cup of Greek yoghurt and 1 and 3/4 of self-raising flour to a mixing bowl with a half a teaspoon of salt. Mix with your hands until you have a fluffy dough (it shouldn't stick to your hands so add more flour if it does).
2. Sprinkle some flour onto a worktop, place your dough down and divide into 4 balls. Roll each ball out into a thin, long flatbread shape (make sure it'll fit in your frying pan).
3. Heat up some oil in a pan and add the flatbread. Fry on each side for 3 minutes on a medium heat.
4. Add your chicken thigh fillets to a bowl with 1 tablespoon of Greek yoghurt, 1 teaspoon of smoked paprika, 1 teaspoon of cumin, 1 teaspoon of cajun seasoning and 3 cloves of crushed garlic with some salt and pepper.
5. Place your chicken thighs in the air fryer for 12 minutes on 200 degrees or in the oven in a roasting dish for 35 minutes with a drizzle of oil.
6. Chop up your onion and add that to a frying pan with some oil and cook for 5 minutes.
7. Make up your smoky dressing for the flatbreads by mixing 2 tablespoons of yoghurt, half a teaspoon of paprika, half a teaspoon of cajun and 1 clove of grated garlic. Spread the dressing over each flatbread.
8. When your chicken is cooked, remove and chop up thinly. Add some chicken and red onion to each flatbread. Tear up your mozzarella and add that too. Finish with some chilli flakes and a garnish of salad if you like.

Air Fryer Orange Chicken From Frozen

Servings: 2
Cooking Time: 15 Minutes

Ingredients:
- 10 ounces (240 g) Frozen Orange Chicken (about 2 cups worth)
- Sauce from the Packaged Frozen Orange Chicken
- EQUIPMENT
- Air Fryer

Directions:
1. Place the frozen orange chicken in the air fryer basket and spread out into a single even layer. No oil spray is needed. Set the sauce aside (do not sauce the chicken yet).
2. Air Fry at 400°F/205°C for 8 minutes. Shake and flip the chicken pieces over and then continue to cook at 400°F/205°C for another 2-4 minutes or until heated through and crispy.
3. Warm the orange sauce in microwave for 1 minute or on stovetop for 2-3 minutes on medium heat. Toss cooked chicken with sauce and serve.

NOTES

Air Frying Tips and Notes:

No Oil Necessary. Cook Frozen - Do not thaw first.

Shake or turn if needed. Don't overcrowd the air fryer basket.

Recipe timing is based on a non-preheated air fryer. If cooking in multiple batches of orange chicken back to back, the following batches may cook a little quicker.

Recipes were tested in 3.7 to 6 qt. air fryers. If using a larger air fryer, the orange chicken might cook quicker so adjust cooking time.

Remember to set a timer to shake/flip/toss as directed in recipe.

Air Fryer Chicken Stuffed With Prosciutto And Fontina

Servings: 2
Cooking Time: 25 Minutes

Ingredients:
- 2 skinless boneless chicken breast halves
- 4 ounces fontina cheese, rind removed, cut into 2-inch sticks
- 2 slices prosciutto
- salt, to taste
- freshly ground black pepper, to taste
- 4 tablespoons unsalted butter
- 2 tablespoons extra-virgin olive oil
- 1 cup portobello mushrooms, sliced
- 1/2 cup dry white wine
- 3 sprigs rosemary
- 1 bunch baby arugula
- 1/2 lemon, juiced

Directions:
1. Place chicken breast halves between sheets of wax paper, and using a mallet or rolling pin, pound thin.
2. Wrap each fontina cheese stick with one slice prosciutto and place in center of each flattened chicken breast half. Roll chicken around prosciutto and cheese and secure with toothpicks or butcher's twine. Season chicken rolls with salt and black pepper.
3. In a heavy skillet, heat 2 tablespoons of the butter and 1 tablespoon of the olive oil. Quickly brown chicken rolls over medium heat, 2 to 3 minutes per side. Place chicken rolls in air fryer basket. Set air fryer temperature to 350 degrees, and air fry for 7 minutes. Remove chicken rolls to a cutting board and let rest for 5 minutes. Cut rolls at an angle into 6 slices.
4. Reheat skillet, add remaining butter, mushrooms, wine, and rosemary; season with salt and black pepper; and simmer for 10 minutes.
5. In a large bowl, toss arugula leaves in remaining olive oil, lemon juice, salt, and pepper. To serve, arrange chicken and mushrooms on bed of dressed arugula.

Chipotle, Honey & Lime Wings

Servings: 2

Ingredients:
- 700g chicken wings
- 2 tsp Cape Herb & Spice Chipotle Seasoning
- 1 1/2 tsp baking powder
- 1/2 tsp salt
- Sauce
- 2 Tbsp honey
- 1 Lime
- 1 tsp Cape Herb & Spice Chipotle Seasoning
- Spice
- Garnish
- (optional)
- Fresh Coriander
- 1 Spring Onion, thinly sliced

Directions:
1. Start by preparing the chicken wings. Cut the wingtip from the wings, and cut the wing in half at the joint to create 2 winglets. Repeat with all the wings. Toss the wings with chipotle seasoning, baking powder, and salt.
2. The wings can be cooked now, but for optimal extra crispy results, place the wings on a cooling rack over a baking sheet, and place them uncovered in the fridge for 8 hours - 24 hours, to dry out.
3. Once ready to cook preheat the Instant Vortex to 202C, for 25 minutes on air fry. Place the wings in an even layer in the fryer basket, then cook until golden and crisp, shaking halfway through.

Air Fried Chicken

Servings: 2

Ingredients:
- 2 chicken legs
- 2 chicken thighs (bone-in, skin on)
- 1 cup buttermilk
- 1½ cups all-purpose flour
- 1 teaspoon garlic powder
- 1 teaspoon onion powder
- 1 teaspoon paprika
- 1 teaspoon salt
- ½ teaspoon black or white pepper
- Oil spray
- Items Needed
- Cooling rack
- Sheet tray

Directions:
1. Combine chicken legs, thighs, and buttermilk in a resealable plastic bag. Marinate for 1–1½ hours.
2. Mix the flour and all spices in a bowl.
3. Remove chicken legs and thighs straight from the bag and dredge in the flour mixture, making sure the chicken is completely covered.
4. Place the coated chicken on a cooling rack fitted over a sheet tray and let rest at room temperature for 15 minutes.
5. Place the crisper plate into the Smart Air Fryer basket, then place the breaded chicken legs and thighs onto the crisper plate. Spray them generously on all sides with oil spray.
6. Select the Chicken function, adjust temperature to 390°F and time to 17 minutes, then press Start/Pause.
7. Remove the chicken when done and let cool for 5 minutes.
8. Serve warm.

5 Ingredient Crispy Cheesy Air Fryer Chicken Dinner Recipe

Servings: 4
Cooking Time: 8 Minutes

Ingredients:
- 4 thin chicken breasts or two chicken breasts cut/pounded to be thin
- 1 cup milk
- [1/2 cup panko bread crumbs]
- 3/4-1 cup shaved Parmesan-Asiago cheese blend can use any type of hard shaved or shredded cheese like Parmesan, Asiago, Romano
- salt + pepper to taste

Directions:
1. Preheat your air fryer to 400 degrees. Spray the cooking basket lightly with cooking spray.
2. In a large bowl place the milk and chicken breasts. Sprinkle in a generous pinch of salt and freshly ground pepper. Allow to marinate in the milk for 10 minutes.
3. In a shallow bowl combine panko bread crumbs and shaved cheese.
4. Dredge chicken breasts through panko and cheese mixture (press the mixture on top of the chicken generously) and place in the air fryer basket. Make sure that the basket is not overcrowded. I fit 2 chicken breasts in the basket, so I did this in two batches. Spray the top of the chicken lightly with cooking spray (this 'locks on' the cheesy bread crumb topping).
5. Cook for 8 minutes, flipping the chicken breasts halfway through.
6. Remove from the air fryer, repeat the process with any remaining chicken breasts. If you want to warm everything, you can add the already cooked chicken breasts into the basket and cook them for 1 minute to warm them! Enjoy

Air Fryer General Tso's Chicken

Servings: 4
Cooking Time: 10 Minutes

Ingredients:
- 1 lb chicken breast boneless, skinless chicken breast or thighs, cut into 1-2 inch pieces
- 1 tbsp cornstarch
- ½ tsp salt
- ¼ tsp black pepper
- ¼ cup General Tso's Sauce
- Garnish: Chopped green onions, sesame seeds
- Homemade General Tso's Sauce:
- ⅓ cup rice wine or vinegar
- ¼ cup hoisin or teriyaki sauce
- 1 tsp red pepper flakes
- 1 tsp fresh garlic minced
- 1 tsp fresh ginger grated
- 1 tbsp granulated sugar
- 2 tbsp cornstarch

Directions:
1. In a medium shallow bowl, toss chicken pieces with cornstarch, salt and pepper, on both sides.
2. Place into the air fryer basket, that is lightly sprayed with nonstick spray.
3. Air fry at 380 degrees F for 8-10 minutes, tossing chicken halfway through cooking time. Chicken should be crispy and have an internal temperature of 165 degrees F.
4. Add sauce to chicken and toss in an air fryer basket. Return basket to air fryer and air fryer at 380 degrees F for 1-2 minutes. Serve with rice or broccoli.
5. To make Homemade General Tso's Sauce:
6. In a medium saucepan, add rice wine or vinegar, hoisin or teriyaki sauce, pepper flakes, garlic and ginger. Stir until fragrant.
7. Add in sugar, then stir together until sugar dissolves and sauce begins to lightly boil.
8. Remove from heat and add cornstarch.
9. Continue whisking until the sauce thickens.

NOTES
Variations
Use different sauce ingredients - While this air fryer general Tso's chicken recipe is perfect as is, you can always change the sauce and change the flavor. You can add spicy flavor with chili flakes or any other spicy sauce you like. Adding soy sauce is also a great way to add a different flavor.

BEEF, PORK & LAMB RECIPES

Air Fryer Beef Jerky

Ingredients:
- 2 pounds flank steak
- 1/2 cup low-sodium soy sauce
- 2 tablespoons Worcestershire sauce
- 2 teaspoons coarsely-ground black pepper
- 1 teaspoon liquid smoke
- 1 teaspoon onion powder
- 1 teaspoon seasoned salt
- 1/2 teaspoon garlic powder

Directions:
1. Thinly slice the steak into 1/8-inch thick strips, either with the grain (which will result in a chewier beef jerky) or against the grain (which will be more tender). We recommend popping the steak in the freezer for 15-30 minutes before slicing so that it is easier to cut.
2. Transfer the strips of steak to a large ziplock bag.
3. In a separate small mixing bowl, whisk together the remaining ingredients until combined. Pour the mixture into the ziplock bag with the steak, seal the bag, and toss until the steak is evenly coated.
4. Refrigerate for at least 30 minutes or up to 1 day
5. To Dehydrate - Lay the strips out in a single layer on the trays. Dehydrate at 160 degrees for 4-6 hours depending on the thickness and desired texture. (But cooking times will vary based on the thickness of your meat).
6. Remove jerky and transfer to a sealed container. Refrigerate up to 1 month.

Beef Wellingtons And Hasselback Potatoes

Servings: 2
Cooking Time: 30 Minutes

Ingredients:
- Wellingtons:
- 2 Tbsp vegetable oil
- 400g beef fillet, portioned into 200g each if making individual Wellingtons
- Salt and pepper
- 2 Tbsp Dijon mustard
- 1 small onion, finely chopped
- 250g portabellini mushrooms, finely chopped
- 2 Tbsp balsamic vinegar
- 1 tsp dried mixed herbs
- 1 sheet puff pastry, thawed
- 4 slices parma ham
- 1 large egg, beaten
- 2 Tbsp sesame seeds
- Hasselback potatoes
- 4 medium potatoes, washed
- 1/2 cup melted butter
- 3 cloves garlic, crushed
- 1 tsp chopped parsley
- 1 tsp chopped thyme
- 1 tsp chopped rosemary
- 1/2 tsp salt
- 1/4 tsp pepper

Directions:
1. Coat the fillets in 1 tablespoon oil and generously season. Brown the meat on all sides over medium high heat using the Sauté function of your Instant Pot. Remove from the heat, brush each fillet with a tablespoon of mustard and set aside to cool.
2. Add the remaining tablespoon oil to the same pan and add the onion and mushrooms, stirring occasionally to release the water and allowing the mix to brown. Season, add balsamic vinegar and herbs and stir through. Remove from the heat and set aside to cool.
3. For the potatoes, thinly slice the potatoes without going all the way through to the bottom, using 2 wooden spoons or chopsticks on either side of the potato as a guide. In a small bowl combine melted butter, garlic, herbs, salt and pepper and brush generously over each potato and in between each slice.

4. To prepare the wellingtons, on a floured surface, roll out to 3mm thick and if making two portions cut the pastry sheet in half ensuring the pastry is big enough to cover the fillet.
5. Place parma ham in the centre leaving a 1,5cm border. Add 2 tablespoons of the cooled mushroom mix in the middle of the pastry, place the fillet on top and cover all sides with more mushroom mix.
6. Fold over the pastry to cover completely, crimping the edges with a fork if preferred.
7. Score the tops, brush with beaten egg and sprinkle with sesame seeds. Repeat with the other fillet, if using. Refrigerate until ready to cook, at least for 10 minutes.
8. Set the Vortex Plus Clear Cook to ROAST at 200°C degrees for 30 minutes. Add the potatoes first and the wellingtons at 20 minutes. The internal temperature of the steak should read 60 - 65°C for medium rare (it will continue to cook as it rests).
9. Rest the wellingtons for 15 minutes before serving with hasselback potatoes and green vegetables.

Crispy Pork Belly

Servings: 4 - 6

Cooking Time: 30 Minutes Directions:
1. Start by marinating the lamb ribs. Mix the garlic, half the lemon zest, half the lemon juice, olive oil, and spice rub together. Massage the marinade into the lamb ribs and allow them to marinate for at least 30 minutes and ideally overnight.
2. Set the steaming rack (trivet) inside your inner pot and add 1 cup water. Layer the ribs on top of the rack. Secure the lid and set to Pressure Cook on High for 10 minutes.. Once cooked, let the pressure naturally release for 10 minutes, before releasing any remaining pressure.
3. While the lamb ribs cook, chop the mint and parsley together, until fine. Reserve 1 Tbsp of chopped herbs for garnish. Place the remaining chopped herbs in a bowl, along with the remaining lemon zest, lemon juice, garlic, and olive oil.
4. Preheat the Instant Vortex to 191C, on the Roast function for 5 minutes. Once heated place the lamb ribs in the fryer basket, then cook for 5 minutes or until golden, and deliciously soft. Turn and cook on the other side if needed.
5. Spoon the herb sauce over the lamb ribs and serve immediately with a few extra lemon slices.

Air Fryer Ham

Servings: 4
Cooking Time: 35 Minutes

Ingredients:
- 1 small fully cooked ham about 3 pounds
- Glaze
- 2 tablespoons brown sugar
- 1 tablespoon honey
- 1 tablespoon orange juice or pineapple juice
- 1 teaspoon dry mustard

Directions:
1. Preheat air fryer to 320°F.
2. Wrap ham in foil, ensuring that the seam is at the top so it can be opened.
3. Place the wrapped ham in the air fryer and cook 25 minutes.
4. While ham is cooking, combine glaze ingredients.
5. After 25 minutes, unwrap the ham and drizzle glaze over top.
6. Place back in the air fryer (close seam again) and cook an additional 10-15 minutes or until ham reaches 135-140°F.
7. Fold the foil down and cook the ham an additional 5-10 minutes or unti the glaze is browned and the ham reaches 145°F. Rest 10 minutes before serving.

Notes
No Air Fryer? No Problem! We use this recipe to bake ham in the oven. It can also be cooked in a slow cooker.

If your ham is too tall to fit into your air fryer, it can be sliced before wrapping in foil. If slicing the ham before cooking, you may need to reduce cook time.

Air fryers can vary, this recipe was tested in a Cosori 5.8qt air fryer. Check your ham early so it doesn't overcook and dry out. Use a meat thermometer to ensure it doesn't overcook.

SHAPE MATTERS! A thinner flatter shaped ham will need less time than a rounder football shaped ham.

Prunes In Bacon

Servings: 10

Ingredients:
- 500g pitted prunes (45 pieces)
- 23 slices bacon (3 mm thick)

Directions:
1. Cut the slices of bacon in half and wrap each prune with the cut slice. Pierce with a toothpick to hold together.
2. Insert crisper paniere in pan and pan in unit. Select AIR FRY, set temperature to 200°C, and set time to 13 minutes. Press START/STOP to begin and allow to preheat for 3 minutes.
3. After the unit has preheated, place the prunes with bacon on the crisper paniere in the pan and reinsert the pan into the main unit.
4. Remove pan from unit after 2 minutes and shake prunes or toss them with silicone-tipped tongs. Reinsert pan to resume cooking.
5. After 8 minutes, place the prunes on a serving dish to enjoy right away.
6. TIP You can soak the prunes for 30 minutes in cider before wrapping them with the bacon for added flavour.

Roasted Cauliflower Steaks

Servings: 4
Cooking Time: 30 Minutes

Ingredients:
- 2 medium-large heads of cauliflower
- Marinade
- 2 tbsp oil
- 2 tbsp soy sauce (gluten-free if needed)
- 1 tbsp balsamic vinegar
- 1/2 tbsp maple syrup
- 3/4 tsp ground cumin
- 1/2 tsp smoked paprika
- Salt and pepper to taste
- Pinch of cayenne pepper (optional)
- Breading
- 1/2 cup (60 g) chickpea flour or oat flour
- 3 tbsp nutritional yeast
- 1 tsp paprika
- 1/2 tsp smoked paprika
- Salt and pepper

Directions:
1. You can watch the video in the post for visual instructions.
2. Trim the stem and remove the leaves from the cauliflower heads. Do not remove too much of the stem, otherwise, your "steaks" will fall apart.
3. With a large knife, cut the cauliflower lengthwise through the center into 1 1/2-inch (4 cm) thick pieces. Depending on the thickness of the stem you might end up with 2 or 3 "steaks". Don't throw away the little cauliflower pieces which aren't connected to the stem, use them as well to make cauliflower "wings".
4. Add some water with salt to a large pot and bring to a boil over high heat. Once the water boils, add the cauliflower, cover the pot and cook the cauliflower for 4-5 minutes to soften it a little. After 4-5 minutes, remove the cauliflower and set aside. You can also steam the cauliflower instead of cooking it.

5. In a small bowl mix together oil, soy sauce, balsamic vinegar, maple syrup, cumin, smoked paprika, salt, and pepper to taste.
6. Preheat oven to 410 degrees Fahrenheit (210 degrees Celsius) and line a large baking sheet with parchment paper.
7. Prepare the breading by simply mixing all ingredients (chickpea flour, nutritional yeast, paprika, smoked paprika, salt, and pepper) in a bowl with a whisk.
8. Place cauliflower steaks on the lined baking sheet. Brush with the marinade from all sides (see pictures above in the blog post).
9. Dip the cauliflower steaks in the breading and coat from all sides. Then spray with some cooking spray for a crispy breading.
10. Bake for about 25-30 minutes, or until golden brown, crispy, and fork-tender. Flip cauliflower steaks after 15-20 minutes.
11. Transfer to a platter and serve with fresh herbs, lemon juice, and your favorite dip. I made a cashew tahini dip (check the notes below for the recipe). Enjoy!

Notes
Enjoy the cauliflower steaks with this delicious tahini dressing.
Mix the ingredients for the dip in a small bowl with a whisk until creamy. If needed, add more water to thin out.
Recipe serves 4. Nutrition facts are for one serving.

Air Fryer Bacon Wrapped Avocado

Servings: 4
Cooking Time: 10 Minutes

Ingredients:
- 2 avocados whole
- 1 lb bacon

Directions:
1. Peel and remove avocado pits, then peel and remove skins.
2. Slice avocados into equal size wedges.
3. Wrap each wedge with a slice of bacon, covering the entire wedge.
4. Place wedges with the end piece of the bacon face down in the air fryer basket.
5. Air fry at 380 degrees F for 10-12 minutes until bacon is crispy and cooked to your desired doneness.

NOTES
Variations
Add toppings - I love squeezing a bit of fresh lime juice on top of the large avocados once they're cooked. You can also add cheddar cheese, BBQ sauce, or even diced red peppers and onion. Add extra seasoning - These avocado slices would be delicious with a little bit of garlic powder or a combination of dry rubs.

Spicy Air Fryer Pork Belly With Kabocha Squash

Servings: 2

Ingredients:
- Deselect All
- Gochujang Sauce:
- 2 tablespoons gochujang (Korean red chile paste)
- 1 tablespoon toasted sesame oil
- 1 teaspoon mirin
- 1 teaspoon soy sauce
- 1 teaspoon sugar
- 1 clove garlic, finely grated
- Pork Belly and Squash:
- 1/2 kabocha squash (about 1 1/4 pounds), seeds removed and quartered into wedges
- Nonstick cooking spray
- Kosher salt and freshly ground black pepper
- 1 piece skinless pork belly (about 1 pound)
- 1 scallion, thinly sliced on bias
- Toasted sesame seeds, for sprinkling
- Cooked white rice, for serving

Directions:
1. Special equipment: a 6-quart air fryer
2. Preheat a 6-quart air fryer to 375 degrees F.
3. For the gochujang sauce: Stir together the jarred gochujang, sesame oil, mirin, soy sauce, sugar and garlic in a small bowl; set aside.

4. For the pork belly and squash: Spray the kabocha squash with cooking spray and season with 1/4 teaspoon salt. Set aside.
5. Season the pork belly with 1/2 teaspoon salt and pepper. Place the pork belly in the basket of a 6-quart air fryer, then spray it lightly with cooking spray. Air fry until the pork belly browns and crisps on top and around the edges, about 25 minutes. Flip the pork belly over with cooking tongs and then arrange the kabocha squash around the perimeter. Cook until the pork belly is crisp all over and the squash is tender and charred, about 20 minutes. Brush the pork belly with the gochujang sauce, letting any excess run off. Cook until the sauce is slightly sticky and charred, 3 to 4 minutes more.
6. Remove the pork belly onto a plate and let rest for 10 minutes (the squash can keep warm in the air fryer). Cut into 1/4- to 1/2-inch-thick slices and brush with more sauce, if desired. Sprinkle the scallion and sesame seeds over the pork belly and serve with the squash, rice and remaining sauce.

Brussels & Bacon Flatbread

Ingredients:
- 4-6 slices thick-cut bacon, diced
- 8 ounces Brussels Sprouts, thinly-sliced
- 1/2 of a small red onion, thinly sliced
- 2 cloves garlic, minced
- 2 pieces flatbread (or store-bought naan)
- 1 tablespoon olive oil
- 1 cup Mozzarella cheese, shredded
- Crumbled feta cheese
- Balsamic glaze

Directions:
1. Line a sheet with parchment or foil and lay down the bacon slices. Cook at 350°F for about 10 minutes. Once bacon is at the desired crispiness, set aside to cool.
2. Once the bacon is cooled and able to be handled, dice it into small pieces.
3. Place the piece of flatbread on the 12" circular pizza pan, and brush the top with olive oil. Sprinkle evenly with about 1/3 of the Mozzarella cheese, leaving a 1/2-inch border around the edges of the flatbread. Then add the brussels, red onion, bacon, 1 clove of minced garlic and the crumbled cheese. Finish with a sprinkle more of the mozzarella cheese. Repeat all steps with the second pizza.
4. Bake at 350°F for 8-10 minutes, or until the Mozzarella has melted and the crusts are slightly golden.
5. Remove from the oven and drizzle with the balsamic glaze. Serve immediately.

Air-fryer Beef Wellington Wontons

Servings: 3-1/2
Cooking Time: 10 Minutes

Ingredients:
- 1/2 pound lean ground beef (90% lean)
- 1 tablespoon butter
- 1 tablespoon olive oil
- 2 garlic cloves, minced
- 1-1/2 teaspoons chopped shallot
- 1 cup each chopped fresh shiitake, baby portobello and white mushrooms
- 1/4 cup dry red wine
- 1 tablespoon minced fresh parsley
- 1/2 teaspoon salt
- 1/4 teaspoon pepper
- 1 package (12 ounces) wonton wrappers
- 1 large egg
- 1 tablespoon water
- Cooking spray

Directions:
1. Preheat air fryer to 325F. In a small skillet, cook and crumble beef over medium heat until no longer pink, 4-5 minutes. Transfer to a large bowl. In the same skillet, heat butter and olive oil over medium-high heat. Add garlic and shallot; cook 1 minute. Stir in mushrooms and wine. Cook until

mushrooms are tender, 8-10 minutes; add to beef. Stir in parsley, salt and pepper.
2. Place about 2 teaspoons filling in the center of each wonton wrapper. Combine egg and water. Moisten wonton edges with egg mixture; fold opposite corners over filling and press to seal.
3. In batches, arrange wontons in a single layer on greased tray in air-fryer basket; spritz with cooking spray. Cook until lightly browned, 4-5 minutes. Turn; spritz with cooking spray. Cook until golden brown and crisp, 4-5 minutes longer. Serve warm.

Air Fryer Meatballs
Servings: 4

Ingredients:
- 1 lb. ground beef
- 1/2 c. bread crumbs
- 1/4 c. freshly grated Parmesan
- 1/4 c. freshly chopped parsley
- 1 large egg
- 2 cloves garlic, minced
- 1 tsp. dried oregano
- Kosher salt
- Freshly ground black pepper
- 3 oz. fresh mozzarella, cut into 16 cubes
- Marinara, for serving

Directions:
1. In a large bowl, combine ground beef, bread crumbs, Parmesan, parsley, egg, garlic, and oregano. Season with salt and pepper.
2. Scoop about 2 tablespoons of meat and flatten into a patty in your hand. Place a cube of mozzarella in the center and pinch meat up around cheese and roll into a ball. Repeat with remaining meat to make 16 total meatballs.
3. Working in batches as needed, place meatballs in basket of air fryer and cook at 370° for 12 minutes.
4. Serve with warmed marinara.

Meat Platter With Pap, Chakalaka, Coleslaw And Corn

Ingredients:
- 1 tablespoon coconut oil
- 4 large, grated carrots
- 1½ fresh chillies (Sliced)
- 1 chopped onion
- 2 chopped garlic heads
- ½ chopped red pepper
- ½ chopped yellow pepper
- ½ chopped green pepper
- 1 can baked beans
- 1 tablespoon paprika
- 1 tsp salt
- 1 tsp black pepper
- 1 tablespoon chicken spice
- 1 chicken stock cube

Directions:
1. Set the Instant pot on sauté mode.
2. Heat oil, add onions, garlic and chillies and sauté until the onions are translucent. Then add the red, green, and yellow pepper and sauté for about 3 minutes.
3. Add chicken stock cube, paprika, salt, pepper and stir. Then add grated carrots, chicken spice and mix well. Let it cook for about 10 minutes then add baked beans, stir for about a minute and then turn off the instant pot and let it cool.

Lamb Kofta & Aubergine Wedges
Servings: 4

Ingredients:
- 400g minced lamb, fridge cold
- 20g fresh breadcrumbs, soaked briefly in cold water and squeezed out
- 1 spring onion, chopped finely
- 1 clove garlic, minced
- 2 tsp Baharat spice mix
- 1 1/2 tbsp finely chopped coriander
- 1 1/2 tbsp finely chopped parsley
- 2 tbsp olive oil
- 2 (approx. 600g) aubergines, each cut into 6 wedges

- 1 tsp salt
- 1 tsp pepper
- To garnish extra roughly chopped parsley and coriander
- To sprinkle Aleppo chilli flakes (optional)
- Oil cooking spray
- To serve warm pitta bread
- 4 20cm soaked wooden skewers

Directions:
1. Begin by mixing the minced lamb, breadcrumbs, spring onion, garlic, Baharat spice and finely chopped coriander and parsley in a bowl. Add salt and pepper. Divide the mixture into four and shape evenly onto each skewer leaving 4cm at the end of the stick
2. Mix the aubergines with the 2 tablespoons of oil and season to taste
3. Insert the crisper plate into the Zone 1 drawer, spray the crisper plate with oil and place the kebabs onto the plate with each one facing in opposite directions as you go so they fit in nicely. Insert the drawer in unit
4. Insert the crisper plate into the Zone 2 drawer and place the aubergines inside. Insert the drawer in unit
5. Select Zone 1, turn the dial to select AIR FRY, set temperature to 200°C and set time to 9 minutes. Select Zone 2, turn the dial to select AIR FRY, set temperature to 200°C and set time to 15 minutes. Select SYNC. Press the dial to begin cooking
6. Carefully give the aubergines a turn at least twice whilst cooking so they brown evenly. Check towards the end. They may need a couple more minutes
7. When cooking is complete, serve hot, with warm pitta. Garnish with roughly chopped parsley and coriander and sprinkled with Aleppo pepper, if desired

Air Fryer Meatloaf Recipe
Servings: 4
Cooking Time: 23 Minutes

Ingredients:
- FOR THE MEATLOAF:
- 1 medium yellow onion
- 2 cloves garlic
- 10 sprigs fresh parsley
- 1 large egg
- 2 tablespoons Worcestershire sauce
- 1 teaspoon kosher salt
- 1/2 teaspoon freshly ground black pepper
- 1/2 cup fine dry breadcrumbs
- 1 1/2 pounds ground beef
- FOR THE GLAZE:
- 1/4 cup ketchup
- 2 tablespoons spicy brown mustard

Directions:
1. Cut 1 medium yellow onion into 1-inch pieces. Place in a food processor fitted with the blade attachment and add 2 garlic cloves and the leaves from 10 fresh parsley sprigs. Pulse until finely chopped, 5 to 6 (1-second) pulses. (Alternatively, use the large holes on a box grater to grate the onion and a chef's knife to finely chop the garlic and parsley.) Transfer to a large bowl.
2. Add 1 large egg, 2 tablespoons Worcestershire sauce, 1 teaspoon kosher salt, and 1/2 teaspoon black pepper to the bowl, and stir to combine. Add 1/2 cup fine dry breadcrumbs and stir to combine. Add 1 1/2 pounds ground beef and mix with your hands until combined. Shape the mixture into 2 (3-inch wide, 6-inch long, and 1 1/2-inch high) loaves.
3. Heat an air fryer to 340F to 350F. Place the meatloaves in the air fryer side-by-side and air fry for 12 minutes. Meanwhile, make the glaze. Place 1/4 cup ketchup and 2 tablespoons spicy brown mustard in a small bowl, and stir to combine.
4. Flip the meatloaves over and air fry until the meatloaf darkens around the edges, about 8 minutes. Brush with half of the glaze. Air

fry until an instant-read thermometer inserted into the center registers at least 165F and the glaze darkens slightly, 3 to 4 minutes more. Spoon the remaining glaze over the top of the meatloaves, slice, and serve.

RECIPE NOTES
Storage: Refrigerate leftovers in an airtight container for up to 3 days.

Air Fryer Corned Beef
Servings: 6-8
Cooking Time: 1 Hour 40 Minutes

Ingredients:
- Pickling packet that came with your corned beef*
- ¼ cup brown mustard
- 1 tablespoon apple cider vinegar
- 4-pound corned beef brisket

Directions:
1. Preheat your air fryer to 360 degrees F.
2. Mix the contents of the pickling packet with the mustard and apple cider vinegar, forming a paste.
3. Set the brisket on a large sheet of aluminum foil sprayed lightly with cooking oil. Brush ⅔ of the mustard paste over the whole brisket, reserving the rest, then fold the foil around the brisket.
4. Place the wrapped brisket in the air fryer basket and cook for 1 hour.
5. When the timer goes off, pull back the foil, baste the brisket with the remaining sauce, and cover. Cook for another 40 minutes.
6. Pull back the foil and cook for 5 minutes at 400 degrees, if you'd like a nice top.

NOTES
* if your corned beef didn't come with a pickling packet, you can use this delicious Spiceology mix or make your own pickling spice and use a few teaspoons

HOW TO COOK FROZEN CORNED BEEF IN THE AIR FRYER:
Prepare corned beef through step 4. Cook for an extra 20 minutes to the second cooking time, bringing the total cook time to 2 hours, 5 minutes

HOW TO REHEAT CORNED BEEF IN THE AIR FRYER:
Preheat your air fryer to 360 degrees.
Place unsliced hunk of corned beef in the air fryer and cook for 8 minutes, until warmed through. Slices will only take 1-2 minutes to warm.

Juicy Air Fryer Meatballs
Servings: 16
Cooking Time: 12 Minutes

Ingredients:
- 1 pound lean ground beef
- ? pound lean ground pork
- ? cup seasoned bread crumbs
- 1 egg
- 2 tablespoons milk
- 2 tablespoons fresh parsley
- 1 tablespoon parmesan cheese grated
- ? teaspoon Italian seasoning
- ? teaspoon onion powder
- ? teaspoon salt
- ? teaspoon black pepper

Directions:
1. Combine all ingredients except beef and pork in a medium bowl. Mix well.
2. Add beef and pork and mix to combine. Divide into 16 meatballs.
3. Preheat air fryer to 400F.
4. Place meatballs in a single layer in the air fryer. Turn air fryer down to 380F.
5. Cook meatballs for 12-14 minutes or until browned and the center of the meatball reaches 165F.
6. Rest 3 minutes before serving.

Notes
Air Fryers can vary slightly, check your meatballs a couple of minutes early to ensure they don't overcook. The meatballs should be 165F in the center.
Keep leftover meatballs in an airtight container or a zippered bag in the fridge for up to 4 days and in the freezer for up to a month.

Air Fryer Mexican Pizza

Servings: 2
Cooking Time: 10 Minutes

Ingredients:
- ½ lb ground beef
- 1 tbsp taco seasoning
- 4 flour tortillas
- 1 tsp oil
- 4 tbsp refried beans
- ½ cup salsa
- 1 cup red enchilada sauce
- 1½ cups sharp cheddar jack cheese shredded
- 2 tbsp black olives
- 1 Roma tomato diced
- optional toppings shredded lettuce, green onions, sour cream

Directions:
1. In a small skillet, brown the ground beef until no longer pink. Stir in the taco seasoning until combined, and remove from heat.
2. Use a small skillet and heat the skillet over medium-high heat. Lightly brown the tortillas about 1 minute per side, or until lightly browned and slightly crispy. Set aside. (You can also heat the tortillas in the air fryer. Add the tortillas to the basket of the air fryer and then add a trivet to the top to keep them from flying around. Heat the air fryer to 370 degrees Fahrenheit and air fryer for 3 minutes. Carefully remove the trivet, it will be hot)
3. Place a tortilla into the basket of the air fryer. Spread the top of the tortilla with refried beans. Top the beans with taco meat and with salsa.
4. Add the second tortilla on top of the first. Cover the top of the tortilla with enchilada sauce, diced tomatoes, shredded cheese, green onions, and black olives. Then top with additional shredded cheese.
5. Air fry the Mexican pizza at 370 degrees Fahrenheit for 2-3 minutes. Use a spatula to carefully remove the pizza from the air fryer to a serving plate. Top with lettuce, sour cream, and green onion tops before serving. Repeat the process for the second pizza.

NOTES

I make this recipe in my Cosori 5.8 qt. air fryer or 6.8 quart air fryer. Depending on your air fryer, size and wattages, cooking time may need to be adjusted 1-2 minutes.

If you want to have crispy tortillas for this recipe, you must stick to flour. This copycat version relies on the crispiness of the tortillas to hold sturdy for all those toppings!

Air Fryer Lemon And Herb Pork Schnitzels

Servings: 4
Cooking Time: 40 Minutes

Ingredients:
- 1/2 cup (75g) plain flour
- 2 eggs
- 1/3 cup (80ml) milk
- 2 cloves garlic, crushed
- 2 cups (150g) fresh breadcrumbs
- 1/3 cup (25g) finely grated parmesan
- ¼ cup chopped chives
- 1 tablespoon finely chopped lemon thyme
- 2 teaspoon finely grated lemon rind
- 500 grams thin pork leg steaks
- olive oil cooking spray
- to serve: extra lemon thyme, sea salt flakes, aioli, chips and lemon wedges

Directions:
1. Place flour in a shallow bowl. Lightly beat eggs, milk and garlic in a second shallow bowl. Combine breadcrumbs, parmesan, chives, thyme and lemon rind in a third shallow bowl. Dust pork in flour, shaking off excess, dip in egg mixture, then coat in breadcrumb mixture. Place schnitzels on a plate. Refrigerate for 30 minutes.
2. Preheat a 7-litre air fryer to 180°C/350°F for 3 minutes.

3. Spray schnitzels generously on both sides with cooking spray. Taking care, place half the schnitzels in the air fryer basket; at 180°C/350°F, cook for 10 minutes, turning halfway through cooking time, until golden and cooked through. Transfer to a plate; cover loosely with foil to keep warm. Repeat cooking with remaining schnitzels.
4. Serve schnitzels sprinkled with extra thyme and salt flakes, with aioli, chips and lemon wedges.

Air Fryer Bacon

Ingredients:
- Bacon

Directions:
1. Place bacon in the air fryer.
2. Set the temperature at 400 degrees, and set the timer for 5-8 minutes.
3. Check it halfway through to see if anything needs to be rearranged. Enjoy!

Bacon Wrapped Brussel Sprouts

Ingredients:
- 1/3 cup soy sauce
- ¼ tsp pepper
- ¼ tsp garlic powder
- 8 slices of bacon
- 16 Brussel sprouts

Directions:
1. In a small mixing bowl, whisk together the soy sauce, pepper and garlic powder.
2. Slice the Brussel sprouts in half lengthwise. Place them in the marinade and let them sit for 20 minutes covered.
3. Get your skewers and stick the end of a piece of bacon through the skewer. Add a Brussel sprout, fold the bacon over the Brussel sprout and onto the skewer. Repeat with three more Brussel sprouts, ending with bacon. Repeat these steps until all the Brussel sprouts and bacon are used.
4. Place your skewers onto the air fryer kebab rack and place the rack in the air fryer. Air fry them at 350°F for 5 minutes, flip them and air fry for an additional 4-5 minutes.

How To Make Bacon In The Air Fryer

Servings: 12
Cooking Time: 8 Minutes

Ingredients:
- 1 package of thick cut bacon

Directions:
1. Line the outer basket with aluminum foil and pre-heat the air fryer to 390F. You can also add 1-2 slices of bread to the bottom basket to soak up the grease.
2. Cut the bacon slices in half (or don't, this is optional) and arrange them in the basket in a flat layer. Cook the bacon 5 minutes, then flip and cook for another 3-4 minutes depending on how you like your bacon. If you like it extra crispy, cook it for 4-5 minutes after flipping (total time 8-10 mins). When finished, remove the bacon strips from the air fryer and transfer to a paper towel lined plate.

Notes
This is my favorite air fryer, it holds almost an entire package of bacon!
If you don't have a good pair of tongs to use with an air fryer, check these out - they won't scratch the coating off your air fryer basket.
If you are doing more than one batch, be sure and empty the grease from the lower basket before cooking the second batch.
I prefer thick cut bacon, but you can use thin sliced bacon too. If you are using thinner cuts, watch closely because you may need less time.

Air Fryer Full English

Servings: 4
Cooking Time: 20 Minutes

Ingredients:
- 8 bacon medallions
- 4 reduced fat pork sausages
- 4 medium eggs beaten
- 420 g tin of baked beans
- 200 g cherry tomatoes
- 200 g button mushrooms
- low calorie cooking spray
- salt and pepper to taste

Directions:
1. Pre-heat your air fryer to 180°C.
2. Take a sheet of foil and place the mushrooms onto it. Spray with low calorie cooking spray and season with salt and pepper. Scrunch the edges together to seal it into a pouch. It should look like a pasty that has been stood up.
3. Take a sheet of foil and place the tomatoes onto it. Spray with low calorie cooking spray and season with salt and pepper. Scrunch it into a pouch.
4. Place the sausages and foil pouches into the air fryer for 5 minutes.
5. After 5 minutes, add the bacon medallions. You will need to overlap them to fit in most air fryers - this is fine!
6. After another 5 minutes, open the air fryer and push the bacon into a pile to make room. Add two small ovenproof bowls, one with the baked beans and one with the beaten eggs. Close the air fryer and cook for another 5 minutes.
7. Open the air fryer again and mix the eggs with a fork, close the lid and cook for a further 2 minutes.
8. Turn off the air fryer and mix up the eggs. Plate up the breakfasts and serve!

Frozen Pork Chops In The Air Fryer

Servings: 4
Cooking Time: 15 Minutes

Ingredients:
- 4 1-inch thick boneless pork chops, frozen
- 1 ½ teaspoons smoked paprika
- 1 teaspoon brown sugar
- ½ teaspoon kosher salt
- ½ teaspoon black pepper
- ¼ teaspoon onion powder
- ¼ teaspoon garlic powder
- ⅛ teaspoon cayenne pepper

Directions:
1. Preheat your air fryer to 380 degrees F.
2. Place the frozen chops in the air fryer in a single layer. Defrost the chops in the air fryer for 5 minutes.
3. While the chops defrost, mix together the remaining ingredients in a small bowl.
4. When the timer is done, open the basket and remove the chops to a cutting board. Spray them with cooking spray, then sprinkle the dry rub on all over the chops.
5. Return the chops to the fryer basket and continue cooking for 12-18 minutes (depending on the thickness of your chops), or until the middle is no longer pink, and reads 145 degrees F when probed with a meat thermometer.
6. Allow the chops to rest for 5 minutes before serving.

NOTES
HOW TO REHEAT PORK CHOPS IN THE AIR FRYER:
Preheat your air fryer to 350 degrees.
Place the leftover pork chops in the air fryer and cook for 3 to 5 minutes, until they're thoroughly warmed.

FISH & SEAFOOD RECIPES

Salmon Catnip Cat Treats

Servings: 20

Ingredients:
- 1 can skinless or boneless tuna or salmon packed in water (6 ounces)
- ¼ cup fresh catnip flowers

Directions:
1. Drain the tuna or salmon and add to a bowl.
2. Chop the catnip flowers into ¼-inch-thick pieces. Discard any stems.
3. Mix the fish with the catnip until combined.
4. Shape the mixture into 1-inch-wide patties, about ⅛-inch-thick.
5. Place the patties evenly between the Food Dehydrator trays.
6. Set temperature to 145°F and time to 3 hours, then press Start/Stop.
7. Remove the patties when done.
8. Cool to room temperature on the trays.
9. Break into smaller treat-sized pieces and serve or store in an airtight container.

Air Fryer Salmon With Skin

Servings: 3
Cooking Time: 7 Minutes

Ingredients:
- 3 Salmon fillets
- 1 Tablespoon Olive oil substitute with any other flavourless oil of choice
- 1 teaspoon smoked paprika substitute with sweet paprika
- 1 teaspoon garlic granules substitute with freshly minced garlic cloves
- 1/2 teaspoon onion granules
- salt and freshly ground black pepper to taste I used less than a teaspoon each
- Lemon wedge to serve

Directions:
1. Preheat the air fryer at 200C/400F for 5 minutes
2. To a small bowl, add smoked paprika, garlic granules, onions granules, salt and black pepper and stir to combine.
3. Pat the salmon dry with a kitchen papper towel. Drizzle the olive oil on the fillets.
4. Sprinkle the fish seasoning on each of the fillets and pat it down into the fish using your hands.
5. Carefully place the salmon in the air fryer basket and cook at 200C/400F for 7 to 8 minutes or until the internal temperature registers 120F/50C. The fish would continue to cook as it rests. You will tknow the fish is done if it flakes apart easily with a fork.
6. Remove it from the air fryer and serve with other sides of choice

NOTES
How to store
Fridge: leave the salmon to cool completely and store in the fridge for up to 3 days in an airtight container.
Freezer: You can freeze the salmon for up to 3 months in an airtight container or a Ziploc freezer bag making sure you take out as much air as possible.

Air Fryer Shrimp

Servings: 4
Cooking Time: 8 Minutes

Ingredients:
- 1 pound medium raw shrimp, peeled and deveined
- 1/2 cup olive oil
- 2 tablespoons lemon juice
- 1 teaspoon black pepper
- 1/2 teaspoon salt

Directions:
1. Preheat your air fryer to 400 degrees.
2. Place the shrimp in a Ziploc bag with olive oil, lemon juice, salt, and pepper. Carefully combine all ingredients.

3. Add parchment paper round (if using) and place the raw shrimp inside the air fryer in one layer.
4. Cook for about 8 minutes, shaking the basket halfway through. The shrimp are done when the shrimp turns bright pink but is still just slightly white, but still a little opaque.
5. Remove the shrimp from the air fryer and enjoy!

NOTES
HOW TO REHEAT SHRIMP IN THE AIR FRYER:
Preheat your air fryer to 350 degrees.
Place the shrimp in the air fryer and cook for 2-3 minutes, until warmed.
Remove the shrimp from the air fryer and enjoy!
HOW TO COOK FROZEN RAW SHRIMP IN THE AIR FRYER:
Preheat you air fryer to 400 degrees.
Place frozen raw shrimp in the air fryer and cook for 8-10 minutes shaking the basket halfway through.
Remove the shrimp from the air fryer and enjoy!
If using precooked frozen shrimp in the air fryer, cook for about 5 minutes until heated thoroughly.

Air Fryer Scallops

Servings: 4
Cooking Time: 5 Minutes

Ingredients:
- 1/2 cup Italian breadcrumbs
- 1/2 teaspoon garlic powder
- 1/4 teaspoon salt
- 1/2 teaspoon black pepper
- 2 tablespoons butter, melted
- 1 pound sea scallops, patted dry

Directions:
1. Preheat your air fryer to 390 degrees F.
2. In a shallow bowl, mix the breadcrumbs, garlic powder, salt, and pepper together. Pour melted butter into a second shallow bowl.
3. Dredge each scallop through the melted butter, then roll in the breadcrumb mixture until they're completely coated; set aside on a plate.
4. Lightly spray the preheated air fryer basket with cooking spray. Arrange scallops in a single layer, working in batches if necessary.
5. Air fry the scallops for 2 minutes. Use tongs to carefully flip them over, then air fry for 3 more minutes until opaque and golden brown.

NOTES
How to Reheat Scallops in the Air Fryer:
Preheat your air fryer to 390 degrees.
Cook leftover sea scallops in the air fryer for 2 to 3 minutes, until warmed thoroughly.
HOW TO COOK FROZEN SCALLOPS IN THE AIR FRYER:
Preheat your air fryer to 390 degrees.
Place frozen scallops in the air fryer and cook for about 7 minutes, flipping them halfway through.

Blackened Air Fryer Salmon Bites

Servings: 4
Cooking Time: 7 Minutes

Ingredients:
- 4 6 ounce skinless salmon filets (diced in 1 inch chunks)
- olive oil spray
- 1 tablespoon sweet paprika
- 1/2 teaspoon dried cayenne pepper
- 1 teaspoon garlic powder
- 1 teaspoon dried thyme
- 1 teaspoon dried oregano
- 1 teaspoon kosher salt
- 1/8 teaspoon black pepper
- lemon wedges (for serving)
- chopped parsley (for garnish)
- brown rice (optional for serving)

Directions:
1. Place salmon in a large bowl and spritz the salmon with oil.
2. Combine all the spices, from paprika to black pepper in a small bowl and mix. Rub all over the salmon.

3. Spray the basket with oil.
4. Place salmon in the air fryer basket and air fry 400F about 5 to 7 minutes, shaking halfway until the salmon is cooked through in the center and browned all over.
5. Serve with lemon wedges and fresh parsley.

Air Fryer Honey Sriracha Salmon

Servings: 4
Cooking Time: 25 Minutes

Ingredients:
- 4 Tbsp. butter, softened
- 3 Tbsp. honey
- 1 ½ tsp. Sriracha
- 1 lime, juiced
- 2 Tbsp. Worcestershire
- 1 ½ Tbsp. minced garlic
- 1 tsp. salt
- ½ tsp. pepper
- 4 (5 oz) salmon fillets

Directions:
1. In a small bowl, whisk together the butter, honey, Sriracha, lime juice, Worcestershire, garlic, salt and pepper.
2. Pat the salmon dry and spread the honey Sriracha mixture over the salmon fillets.
3. Place baking rack in the bowl in the high position and spray with cooking spray. Place two fillets on top.
4. Tap the bake button and set temperature to 400°F and fry for 12-13 minutes. Repeat with remaining fillets.
5. Serve warm with cooked brown rice and an extra squeeze of lime juice.

Air Fryer Mexican Shrimp

Servings: 4
Cooking Time: 10 Minutes

Ingredients:
- 1 lb. white shrimp, peeled, deveined, and tails removed
- 1 tablespoon olive oil
- 1 teaspoon ground cumin
- 1 teaspoon chili powder (optional for a kick)
- 1/2 teaspoon paprika
- 1/2 teaspoon garlic powder
- 1/2 teaspoon dried oregano (or Italian seasoning)
- 1/2 teaspoon salt
- 1/4 teaspoon ground black pepper
- 1 tablespoon fresh cilantro, chopped (optional, for garnish)

Directions:
1. In a medium bowl, add shrimp, olive oil, cumin, chili powder, paprika, garlic powder, oregano, salt and pepper. Toss well to coat and set aside to marinate for 15 minutes (if you have the time).
2. Transfer the shrimp into the air fryer basket. Cook at 350 F for 8-10 minutes, shaking the basket once halfway through.
3. Sprinkle with cilantro on top and serve.

NOTES

How to store: Leftover shrimp will keep in the refrigerator for up to 3-4 days when stored in an airtight container. Allow it to cool to room temperature before placing in the refrigerator.

How to reheat shrimp: Reheat in a skillet over medium-low heat until warmed through, about 5 minutes, or in the microwave for about 1 minute. You can also reheat in a preheated oven or air fryer at 300F for about 5 minutes until warmed through. Reheating can cause the shrimp to be a little drier than when served fresh. You can also eat leftovers cold on a salad.

Alternate cooking methods: You can cook this shrimp in the oven by spreading it evenly on a parchment-lined quarter sheet baking pan and baking in a 400 F preheated oven for 8-10 minutes until the shrimp turns pink. You can also cook over the stovetop by sautéing over medium-high heat for 5 minutes until shrimp turns pink and nicely browned.

Coconut Prawns

Ingredients:
- 15 King prawns
- 1/2 Cup flour
- 2 Tsp salt flakes
- 1 Tsp black pepper
- 1 Tsp garlic powder
- 2 Eggs
- 1/4 Cup coconut
- 1/4 Cup breadcrumbs

Directions:
1. Prepare the prawns by removing the heads, then using kitchen shears, cut the shell down lengthwise to the tail. Remove the shell and legs, leaving the tail. Now use a sharp knife to cut along the centre of the back and remove the vein. Rinse under cold water and pat dry.
2. Place flour, salt, pepper and garlic powder into a bowl. Place the egg into a second bowl and whisk, then place the coconut breadcrumb mixture. Place into the air fryer basket in a single layer and cook for 10 minutes at 200C.
3. Serve with dipping sauce of choice.

Air Fryer Cajun Shrimp Dinner

Servings: 4
Cooking Time: 20 Minutes

Ingredients:
- 1 tablespoon Cajun or Creole seasoning
- 24 (1 pound) cleaned and peeled extra jumbo shrimp
- 6 ounces fully cooked Turkey/Chicken Andouille sausage or kielbasa* (sliced)
- 1 medium zucchini (8 ounces, sliced into 1/4-inch thick half moons)
- 1 medium yellow squash (8 ounces, sliced into 1/4-inch thick half moons)
- 1 large red bell pepper (seeded and cut into thin 1-inch pieces)
- 1/4 teaspoon kosher salt
- 2 tablespoons olive oil

Directions:
1. In a large bowl, combine the Cajun seasoning and shrimp, toss to coat.
2. Add the sausage, zucchini, squash, bell peppers, and salt and toss with the oil.
3. Preheat the air fryer 400F.
4. In 2 batches (for smaller baskets), transfer the shrimp and vegetables to the air fryer basket and cook 8 minutes, shaking the basket 2 to 3 times.
5. Set aside, repeat with remaining shrimp and veggies.
6. Once both batches are cooked, return the first batch to the air fryer and cook 1 minute.

Notes
Tip: Buy shrimp still frozen and defrost as needed. Most shrimp arrives at stores frozen so you may as well buy it frozen and defrost it as needed so it as fresh as possible. To defrost shrimp, thaw overnight in the refrigerator.
*check labels for whole30 and gluten-free.

Air Fryer Frozen Shrimp

Servings: 3
Cooking Time: 10 Minutes

Ingredients:
- 1 pound (454 g) frozen raw shrimp
- oil spray or vegetable oil , to coat shrimp
- salt , to taste
- black pepper , to taste

Directions:
1. Evenly coat the frozen shrimp with oil spray or vegetable oil. Season with salt & pepper (you do not need to thaw the shrimp).
2. Place the frozen shrimp in the air fryer basket and spread in an even layer (make sure they aren't overlapping).
3. Air Fry at 400°F/205°C for 8-14 minutes (depending on the size of your shrimp and your air fryer), flipping the shrimp halfway through cooking. Check for doneness & air fry longer if needed.

NOTES
Air Frying Tips and Notes:
Cook Frozen - Do not thaw first.

Shake or turn if needed. Don't overcrowd the air fryer basket.

If cooking in multiple batches, the first batch will take longer to cook if Air Fryer is not already pre-heated. Recipe timing is based on a non-preheated air fryer.

Recipes were tested in 3.4 to 6 qt air fryers. If using a larger air fryer, the recipe might cook quicker so adjust cooking time.

Remember to set a timer to shake/flip/toss as directed in recipe.

Air Fryer Salmon

Servings: 4
Cooking Time: 10 Minutes

Ingredients:
- 1 pound salmon
- salt and pepper
- 2 tablespoons brown sugar
- 1 teaspoon chili powder
- 1/2 teaspoon paprika
- 1 teaspoon Italian seasoning
- 1 teaspoon garlic powder

Directions:
1. Salt and pepper the salmon. In a small bowl add the brown sugar, chili powder, paprika, Italian seasoning and garlic powder. Rub on the salmon.
2. In the basket of your air fryer add the salmon skin side down. Turn the air fryer to 400 degrees and cook for 10 minutes. If adding asparagus add to the basket after 5 minutes.

Air Fryer Fish

Servings: 4
Cooking Time: 25-55 Minutes

Ingredients:
- FOR THE FISH AND FRENCH FRIES:
- Cooking spray
- 1 pound frozen steak fries
- 1 1/2 cups panko breadcrumbs
- 1 1/2 teaspoons kosher salt, divided
- 1/3 cup all-purpose flour
- 1/4 teaspoon freshly ground black pepper
- 2 large eggs
- 2 tablespoons water
- 4 (6-ounce) skinless cod fillets
- Malt vinegar and lemon wedges, for serving
- FOR THE TARTAR SAUCE:
- 1/2 cup mayonnaise
- 1 teaspoon sweet pickle relish
- 1/2 teaspoon Dijon mustard
- 1/2 teaspoon freshly squeezed lemon juice

Directions:
1. MAKE FISH AND FRENCH FRIES:
2. Heat air fryer to 400°F for 10 minutes. Coat the air fryer basket with cooking spray. Working in batches if needed, place 1 pound frozen steak fries in a single layer in the air fryer basket. Air fry for 6 minutes. Flip the fries and air fry until crispy, 6 to 8 minutes more. (Final cook time will depend on your air fryer's capacity and the thickness of your fries.)
3. Meanwhile, place 1 1/2 cups panko breadcrumbs and 1 teaspoon of the kosher salt in a shallow dish and stir to combine. Place 1/3 cup all-purpose flour, the remaining 1/2 teaspoon kosher salt, and 1/4 teaspoon black pepper in a second shallow dish and stir to combine. In a third shallow dish, lightly whisk together 2 large eggs and 2 tablespoons water.
4. When the fries are ready, transfer to a serving bowl and season with kosher salt. Tent the bowl loosely with aluminum foil to keep warm. Reduce the air fryer temperature to 375°F.
5. Halve 4 cod fillets lengthwise into 2 long strips. (There will be a total of 8 pieces.) Working with one stirp at a time, dredge in the flour mixture and shake off the excess. Dip in the egg mixture and let any excess drip off. Dredge in the panko mixture, pressing it in to adhere. Place on a baking sheet or plate.
6. Working in batches if needed, place the fish in a single layer in the air fryer basket. Air

fry until golden and crispy, flipping halfway through, about 12 minutes total. The thicker parts of the cod fillet will take longer to cook than the thinner parts toward the tail of the fish, so you may need to cook thicker pieces longer. Meanwhile, make the tartar sauce.
7. MAKE THE TARTAR SAUCE:
8. Place 1/2 cup mayonnaise, 1 teaspoon relish, 1/2 teaspoon Dijon mustard, and 1/2 teaspoon lemon juice in a small bowl and whisk to combine.
9. To serve, place 2 pieces of fish and some steak fries on a plate or arrange inside a newspaper cone. Serve with lemon wedges, malt vinegar, and the tartar sauce.
10. RECIPE NOTES
11. Storage: Leftover fish and chips can be refrigerated in an airtight container for up to 2 days. They can be reheated and re-crisped in the air fryer. Heat the air fryer to 350°F for 10 minutes then reheat fish until warmed through, about 5 minutes.

Air Fryer Salmon And Brussels Sprouts

Servings: 4
Cooking Time: 11 Minutes

Ingredients:
- 4 cloves garlic
- 1 teaspoon chopped fresh thyme leaves
- 1 medium lemon
- 2 tablespoons olive oil, divided
- 2 teaspoons kosher salt, divided
- 1 teaspoon freshly ground black pepper, divided
- 4 (7 to 8-ounce) salmon fillets
- Cooking spray
- 1 pound Brussels sprouts
- 1 tablespoon balsamic vinegar
- 1 tablespoon honey

Directions:
1. Mince 4 garlic cloves. Place half in a large bowl and reserve for the Brussels sprouts. Place the remaining garlic in a small bowl. Chop 1 teaspoon fresh thyme leaves, and juice 1 lemon, and add to the small bowl. Add 1 tablespoon of the olive oil, 1 teaspoon of the kosher salt, and 1/2 teaspoon of the black pepper, and whisk to combine. Brush all over the salmon fillets.
2. Preheat an Instant Vortex Plus 7-in-1 Air Fryer Oven to 400°F and set for 10 minutes. Grease the air fryer racks with cooking spray. Place the salmon fillets skin-side down in the bottom rack of the air fryer, leaving space between the fillets.
3. Add the remaining 1 tablespoon olive oil, 1 teaspoon kosher salt, and 1/2 teaspoon freshly ground black pepper to the large bowl with garlic, and stir to combine. Trim and halve 1 pound Brussels sprouts, add to the bowl, and toss to combine. Place in the top rack of the air fryer above the salmon. Air fry until the salmon is cooked to desired doneness, 6 to 8 minutes.
4. Remove the tray of salmon. Continue air frying the Brussels sprouts until golden brown and crispy, 1 to 3 minutes more. Meanwhile, whisk 1 tablespoon balsamic vinegar and 1 tablespoon honey together until combined.
5. Drizzle the honey vinegar over the finished Brussels sprouts before serving.

RECIPE NOTES
Storage: Leftovers can be refrigerated in an airtight container for up to 2 days.
This recipe was tested in the Instant Vortex Plus 7-in-1 Air Fryer Oven. It will work with any air fryer, but timing may differ slightly.

Frozen Salmon In The Air Fryer

Servings: 2
Cooking Time: 15 Minutes

Ingredients:
- 2 6-oz frozen skinless salmon fillets
- 2 teaspoons olive oil
- 1 teaspoon lemon juice
- 1 teaspoon Dijon mustard

- ½ teaspoon kosher salt
- ½ teaspoon garlic powder
- ¼ teaspoon black pepper
- ⅛-¼ teaspoon cayenne pepper
- Lemon wedges, for serving

Directions:
1. Preheat the air fryer to 390 degrees F.
2. In a small bowl, whisk together the olive oil, lemon juice, Dijon, salt, garlic powder, pepper, and cayenne. Brush the mixture on the top of each fillet.*
3. Place the frozen fillets in a single layer inside and cook for 12 to 18 minutes, depending on thickness, until it reaches an internal temperature of 145 degrees F. Serve with lemon wedges if desired.

NOTES
*Alternatively, you can cook the salmon without the seasoning for 6 minutes, then brush it onto the defrosted fillets and continue to cook for 6-12 minutes until cooked through.

Air Fryer Lemon Garlic Shrimp
Servings: 4

Ingredients:
- 1 large garlic clove, grated or minced
- 1 tbsp. extra-virgin olive oil
- 1 tbsp. fresh lemon juice
- 1/2 tsp. Italian seasoning
- 1/4 tsp. crushed red pepper flakes
- 1/4 tsp. kosher salt
- 1/4 tsp. Worcestershire sauce
- 1 lb. large tail-on shrimp (21/25 per lb.), peeled
- 1/2 thinly sliced into half moons, seeds removed
- 2 tbsp. finely chopped fresh parsley

Directions:
1. In a large bowl, whisk garlic, oil, lemon juice, Italian seasoning, red pepper flakes, salt, and Worcestershire. Add shrimp and lemon slices and toss to coat.
2. Working in batches, in an air-fryer basket, arrange shrimp and lemon slices in a single layer (do not overcrowd). Cook at 400° until shrimp are opaque and cooked through, 4 to 6 minutes.
3. Arrange shrimp and lemon slices on a platter. Top with parsley.
4. Make Ahead: Shrimp and lemon slices can be marinated 1 hour ahead. Cover and chill.

Harissa Salmon With Crispy Chickpeas
Servings: 2

Ingredients:
- 230 g (2) salmon fillets
- 3 tbsp Harissa paste, Inspired To Cook
- 1 tbsp olive oil
- 400 g chickpeas
- 1/2 tsp black pepper
- 200 g tenderstem broccoli

Directions:
1. Preheat the air fryer to 180, and prepare the salmon by adding 1 tbsp of harissa paste over each fillet and rub it all over the with the back of a spoon
2. Drain the can of chickpeas, and pour them onto a plate, pat dry with kitchen roll, and pour over the oil, pepper and 1 tbsp of the harissa paste, give them a roll around to combine and pick up all the flavours
3. Add the fillets, and what chickpeas you can fit into the air fryer and fry for 10 minutes finish off the rest of the chickpeas and the broccoli .

Airfried Teriyaki Salmon With Charred Broccoli And Sticky Rice

Ingredients:
- Teriyaki Marinade for 500g protein:
- 4 tbsp soy sauce
- 1 tbsp brown sugar
- 1 tbsp honey
- 2 cloves of garlic grated
- 1 1/2 tsp freshly grated ginger
- 1 tsp rice wine vinegar

Directions:
1. Microwave for 30 seconds so that the honey and sugar dissolves.
2. Coat your fish with 1 tbsp olive oil and season with freshly cracked black pepper. Toss your fish into your marinade and coat well.
3. Preheat your Vortex or Duo Crisp to 205 degC. Set your time for 6 min.
4. When your Vortex prompts you to 'Add Food' then add your fish.
5. Toss your broccoli into the remaining marinade.
6. After 2 min of cooking time add your broccoli to your airfryer.

Notes:
you can use chicken, increase cooking time to 10-12 min depending on the thickness of your chicken. Butterfly your chicken if your fillet is thick

going #wheatfree, replace your soy sauce with Tamari or Coconut Aminos

don't have rice wine vinegar, then replace it with apple cider vinegar

you can reduce or increase your cooking time based on how thick your fish is, or how well done you like it

Crunchy Salmon Circle Cat Treats
Servings: 50
Cooking Time: 4 Hr

Ingredients:
- 1 can boneless, skinless salmon, packed in water (5 ounces)
- ¼ cup water or as needed
- 1 cup oat bran flour or oat flour
- Items Needed
- Food processor
- Parchment paper
- Round cookie cutter (1-inch diameter)

Directions:
1. Drain the canned salmon and place into a food processor. Add the water and blend until the salmon forms a thick paste. If the mixture is too thick, add water, one tablespoon at a time, until the salmon is puréed.
2. Add the salmon paste to a bowl and add the flour. Mix well until you can form a ball with the dough.
3. Place the dough onto a clean work surface lined with parchment paper and roll out to ¼-inch-thick.
4. Cut out the dough into 1-inch circles using a round cookie cutter.
5. Place the dough circles evenly between the Food Dehydrator trays.
6. Set temperature to 145°F and time to 4 hours, then press Start/Stop.
7. Remove the treats when done and crispy and crunchy. Cool completely, then serve to your pet.

Air Fried Popcorn Prawns With Burnt Chilli Mayo
Servings: 4
Cooking Time: 25 Minutes

Ingredients:
- 2 Red Chillies
- 450g Cooked King Prawns
- 100g Flour
- 2 Tbsp Cajun Seasoning
- 2 Eggs
- 250g Golden Breadcrumbs
- 1 Lemon
- Olive Oil
- Salt

Directions:
1. In partnership with Mob.
2. Lightly oil the chillies and chuck it into the air fryer, cook on the highest setting for 6-8 mins until charred and cooked throughout.
3. While the chillies roast in the air fryer, open the prawns and drain any liquid from the pack. Dry the prawns with kitchen paper and set aside.
4. Set up 3 medium-sized bowls. Add the flour to the first along with 2 tbsp Cajun seasoning. Crack the eggs into the next

bowl and beat with a pinch of salt and 1 tbsp of water. Add the breadcrumbs to the final bowl and stir in 1 tbsp of olive oil. It will clump up to begin with, keep stirring to distribute the oil evenly.
5. Working in batches, pass the prawns through each of the bowls, an even dusting of seasoned flour then through the egg mix. Let the excess drain away then toss through the breadcrumbs. Set the breaded prawns to one side. Repeat with the remaining prawns.
6. Remove the chillies from the air fryer and scrape on the charred skin. Remove the seeds and chop into a paste. Stir through the mayo with the zest of the lemon and season to taste.
7. Add the breaded prawns to the air fryer and cook on high for 8 mins until golden brown and crispy. Toss with salt and a little extra Cajun seasoning. Serve with the spicy mayo and cut the lemon into wedges for squeezing.

Air Fryer Fish Sticks

Servings: 3
Cooking Time: 9 Minutes

Ingredients:
- 12 frozen fish sticks

Directions:
1. Preheat your air fryer to 400 degrees.
2. Place frozen fish sticks in the air fryer in one layer not touching.
3. Cook for 9-10 minutes, flipping halfway, until warmed thoroughly.
4. Remove from the air fryer and enjoy!

NOTES
HOW TO REHEAT FISH STICKS IN THE AIR FRYER
Preheat your air fryer to 400 degrees.
Cook leftover fish sticks in the air fryer for 1 to 2 minutes, until fully warmed then enjoy!

Bacon-wrapped Shrimp In Air Fryer

Servings: 3-4
Cooking Time: 10 Minutes

Ingredients:
- 1 pound bacon, thinly sliced
- 1 pound raw jumbo shrimp, peeled and deveined
- ½ cup maple syrup
- 4 tablespoons low sodium soy sauce
- 1 teaspoon garlic powder
- ¼ teaspoon red pepper flakes
- Salt and pepper to taste
- Optional: garnish with green onion

Directions:
1. Cut your bacon slices in half, lengthwise. Wrap one slice of your bacon around your shrimp; start at the tail and overlap the first piece of bacon to help hold it on and then wrap up and around the shrimp with as little overlap as possible till you get to the top of the shrimp. Then lay the wrapped shrimp on a baking sheet.
2. Combine the maple syrup, soy sauce, garlic powder, red pepper flakes, salt, and pepper in a small bowl. Use a basting brush to brush the shrimp with the glaze. Flip the shrimp and coat the other side.
3. Preheat the air fryer to 400 degrees F. Place the shrimp in the air fryer, leaving space around them. Cook for 4 minutes and then flip them. Brush them with more sauce and then continue cooking for about 6 minutes more, or until the bacon is crispy.
4. Serve hot and enjoy.

NOTES
HOW TO REHEAT BACON-WRAPPED SHRIMP IN THE AIR FRYER
Preheat the air fryer to 370 degrees F.
Lay the bacon-wrapped shrimp in the air fryer in a single layer.
Cook for 2 to 3 minutes until heated through.

Air Fryer Bacon Wrapped Scallops

Servings: 4-6
Cooking Time: 12 Minutes

Ingredients:
- 1 pound large sea scallops
- 1 pound center cut slices of bacon
- 3 tablespoons melted butter
- 1/2 teaspoon of old bay seasoning
- salt and pepper to taste
- 1 teaspoon honey
- 1/4 teaspoonred pepper flakes, optional

Directions:
1. Brush your bacon strips with honey. This will help them carmelize in the air fryer and add a slightly sweet flavor.
2. Place your bacon in your air fryer basket. Cook it at 350 degrees for 5-7 minutes. Toss the bacon slices a few times to keep them moving. You will slightly precook it so when you wrap it around your scallop it will fully cook since it takes longer for the bacon than the scallop to cook. It is okay to overlap your bacon. You are not looking to get it crisp at this point, just slightly cooked.
3. Pat your scallops with a paper towel and season with salt and pepper.
4. Wrap your scallops with ½-1 slice of bacon. I was able to wrap most of my scallops with a whole slice of bacon but may have to trim the bottom of the bacon depending on how the scallop is shaped.
5. Hold the bacon in place with a toothpick.
6. Melt your butter and incorporate the old bay seasoning. Brush the butter mixture over your scallops.
7. Cook your scallops at 350 for 11-13 minutes. You do not want to overcook your scallops. The bacon should be crispy and the scallops should be firm but slightly bounce back when you touch it. Optional: sprinkle red pepper flakes over top of them.

Air Fryer Shrimp Tacos

Servings: 6
Cooking Time: 5 Minutes

Ingredients:
- 1 lb shrimp peeled and deveined
- 1 tbsp olive oil
- 1 tsp garlic powder
- 1 tsp paprika
- 1 tsp chili powder
- ½ tsp kosher salt
- ½ tsp cumin
- 6 small tortillas flour or corn
- Cream Sauce
- ½ cup mayonnaise
- ¼ cup sriracha sauce
- 1 tsp fresh lime juice
- Optional toppings
- 1 cup cabbage purple, shredded
- 1 avocado medium, sliced
- 1 cup cotija cheese crumbled
- cilantro garnish

Directions:
1. In a medium bowl, toss shrimp with the olive oil to coat.
2. In a small bowl, stir together the seasonings, then add to the bowl with shrimp. Lightly toss shrimp with seasonings until well coated.
3. Place shrimp in the air fryer basket and air fry at 400 degrees F for 5-7 minutes, until shrimp is cooked.
4. While the shrimp is in the air fryer, in a small bowl, stir together the mayo and hot sauce. Cover and set aside until tacos are assembled.
5. Once the shrimp is done fill tortillas with shrimp, then add additional desired toppings. Drizzle spicy sriracha sauce over tacos before serving.

NOTES
Top Tips
One of the easiest ways to make this simple shrimp taco recipe unique is to have a different taco topping bar every time! All new toppings give all new taste and flavor.

If you want to go simple, you can use some low sodium taco seasoning to create perfect shrimp. You can find it at your local grocery store, and it's a great way to season food fast.

Make this a low carb recipe by skipping the tortillas and just add to lettuce leaves instead. You'll still have that yummy flavor but without the overload of carbs.

Air Fryer Coconut-fried Shrimp With Dipping Sauce

Servings: 4
Cooking Time: 20 Minutes

Ingredients:
- Coconut-Fried Shrimp
- ½ cup all-purpose flour
- 1 teaspoon salt
- ½ teaspoon baking powder
- ⅔ cup water
- 2 cups shredded sweetened coconut
- ½ cup breadcrumbs
- 1 pound medium or large shrimp, peeled and deveined
- oil, for spraying
- Dipping Sauce
- ½ teaspoon crushed red pepper flakes
- 4 teaspoons rice wine vinegar
- ½ cup orange marmalade

Directions:
1. Coconut-Fried Shrimp
2. In a large bowl, whisk together, flour, salt, and baking powder. Add water and whisk until smooth. Let batter stand for 15 minutes. In a shallow bowl, toss together coconut and breadcrumbs. Place shrimp in batter and coat well. Remove shrimp, one at a time, and press into coconut mixture. Coat well.
3. Spray shrimp on all sides with oil and place in air fryer basket in a single layer. Set temperature to 400 degrees, and air fry for 5 minutes. Turn shrimp, spray with oil, and air fry for 5 minutes more. Repeat with remaining shrimp.
4. Dipping Sauce
5. For the dipping sauce, in a medium saucepan, combine red pepper flakes, vinegar, and marmalade and simmer on low heat for 10 minutes, stirring occasionally.

Air-fryer Salmon Cakes

Servings: 2

Ingredients:
- Cooking spray
- 2 (7.5 ounce) cans unsalted pink salmon (with skin and bones)
- 1 large egg
- ½ cup whole-wheat panko breadcrumbs
- 2 tablespoons chopped fresh dill
- 2 tablespoons canola mayonnaise
- 2 teaspoons Dijon mustard
- ¼ teaspoon ground pepper
- 2 lemon wedges

Directions:
1. Coat the basket of an air fryer with cooking spray.
2. Drain salmon; remove and discard any large bones and skin. Place the salmon in a medium bowl. Add egg, panko, dill, mayonnaise, mustard and pepper; stir gently until combined. Shape the mixture into four 3-inch-diameter cakes.
3. Coat the cakes with cooking spray; place in the prepared basket. Cook at 400 degrees F until browned and an instant-read thermometer inserted into the thickest portion registers 160 degrees F, about 12 minutes. Serve with lemon wedges.

Lemon-garlic Air Fryer Salmon

Servings: 2
Cooking Time: 10 Minutes

Ingredients:
- 1 tablespoon melted butter
- ½ teaspoon minced garlic
- 2 (6 ounce) fillets center-cut salmon fillets with skin

- ¼ teaspoon lemon-pepper seasoning
- ⅛ teaspoon dried parsley
- cooking spray
- 3 thin slices lemon, cut in half

Directions:
1. Preheat the air fryer to 390 degrees F (200 degrees C).
2. Combine melted butter and minced garlic in a small bowl.
3. Rinse salmon fillets and dry with a paper towel. Brush with butter mixture and sprinkle with lemon-pepper seasoning and parsley.
4. Spray the basket of the air fryer with cooking spray. Place salmon fillets in the basket, skin-side down, and top each with 3 lemon halves.
5. Cook in the preheated air fryer for 8 to 10 minutes. Remove from the air fryer and let rest for 2 minutes before serving.

Cajun Air Fryer Salmon
Servings: 2
Cooking Time: 10 Minutes

Ingredients:
- cooking spray
- 1 tablespoon Cajun seasoning
- 1 teaspoon brown sugar
- 2 (6 ounce) skin-on salmon fillets

Directions:
1. Gather all ingredients. Preheat the air fryer to 390 degrees F (200 degrees C).
2. Rinse and dry salmon fillets with a paper towel. Mist fillets with cooking spray.
3. Mix together Cajun seasoning and brown sugar in a small bowl until combined; spread onto a plate.
4. Press fillets, flesh-side down, into seasoning mixture.
5. Spray the basket of the air fryer with cooking spray and place salmon fillets skin-side down. Mist salmon again lightly with cooking spray.
6. Close the lid and cook in the preheated air fryer for 8 minutes. Remove from the air fryer and let rest for 2 minutes before serving.

Tips
Increase the cook time by 1 to 2 minutes if you prefer your salmon slightly more done. Do not overcook as it will dry out the salmon.

Striped Bass With Radish Salsa Verde
Servings: 4

Ingredients:
- 1 clove garlic, pressed
- 1 tbsp. anchovy paste or 3 anchovy fillets, finely chopped
- 1/2 small red onion, finely chopped
- 1 tbsp. red wine vinegar
- 1/2 c. plus 1 tbsp. olive oil, divided
- 1 bunch radishes, diced, leaves separated and finely chopped
- 1 c. flat-leaf parsley leaves, finely chopped
- 1 tsp. tarragon leaves, finely chopped
- 4 6-oz fillets striped bass
- Kosher salt and pepper

Directions:
1. In medium bowl, combine garlic, anchovy paste, onion and vinegar and let sit 5 minutes.
2. Stir in 1/2 cup oil, then radishes and greens, parsley and tarragon.
3. Heat remaining tablespoon oil in medium skillet on medium. Pat fish dry and season with 1/2 teaspoon each salt and pepper and cook, skin side down, until skin is crisp and golden brown, about 7 minutes. Flip and cook until fish is opaque throughout, 3 to 6 minutes more. Serve topped with radish salsa verde.

AIR FRYING DIRECTIONS:
4. Heat air fryer to 400°F. Pat fish dry, then brush with remaining 1 tablespoon oil and season with 1/2 teaspoon each salt and pepper. Add to air-fryer basket, skin side down, and air-fry until skin is crispy and fish is opaque throughout, 8 to 10 minutes. Serve topped with radish salsa verde.

SALADS & SIDE DISHES RECIPES

Pita Chips & Hummus
Servings: 4
Cooking Time: 9 Minutes

Ingredients:
- 5 thin pitas
- Spray oil
- Hummus
- 1 can garbanzo beans (15.5 ounces), drained and rinsed
- 1 tablespoon tahini
- 2 garlic cloves, grated
- 3 tablespoons olive oil
- 1 lemon, juiced
- Salt, to taste
- Items Needed
- Food proccessor or blender

Directions:
1. Select the Preheat function on the Air Fryer, adjust the temperature to 370°F, then press Start/Pause.
2. Cut the pitas in half, then cut each half into 4 equal triangles.
3. Place the pita pieces into the preheated air fryer and spray them with oil until they are evenly coated on all sides.
4. Set the temperature to 370°F, time to 9 minutes, then press Start/Pause
5. Shake the basket halfway through the cooking time.
6. Remove the pita chips when done. Let them sit in a bowl for 10 minutes before serving – they will continue to crisp as they cool down.
7. Place the garbanzo beans in a food processor or blender along with the tahini and garlic. Blend until smooth, then add in the olive oil with the motor running. Thin out by blending in with a tablespoon or so of water as needed, if the texture seems too thick. Season the hummus to taste with lemon juice and salt, then serve with the pita chips.

Air Fryer Sauteed Onions
Servings: 2
Cooking Time: 13 Minutes

Ingredients:
- 1 onion
- 1 tablespoon oil
- a small pinch of sugar

Directions:
1. Cut onion into long slices.
2. Heal oil in an air fryer pan on 300 degrees for 1 minute.
3. Place onion slices in the pan and mix evenly to coat the onion with oil.
4. Cook onions on 300 degrees for 5 minutes, stirring halfway through.
5. Add a small pinch of sugar to onions, mix thoroughly, and cook for another 7-10 minutes stirring event 2-3 minutes.
6. Remove pan from air fryer and enjoy with your favorite recipe immediately!

Air Fryer Falafel Salad
Servings: 4

Ingredients:
- 2 cloves garlic
- 4 scallions, whites and greens, thinly sliced, separated
- 6 1/2 c. baby kale, divided
- 2 15-ounce cans chickpeas, drained and rinsed
- 1 tsp. grated lemon zest
- 2 tbsp. all-purpose flour
- 1 tsp. ground cumin
- 1 tsp. ground coriander
- Kosher salt
- 2 tbsp. lemon juice
- 3 tbsp. olive oil, divided, plus more for basket
- 1/2 English cucumber, thinly sliced on bias
- 1/2 c. fresh parsley leaves

- 1/4 c. fresh mint leaves
- Greek yogurt, for topping

Directions:
1. In food processor, pulse garlic, scallion whites, and 1/2 cup baby kale until very finely chopped. Add chickpeas, lemon zest, flour, cumin, coriander, and 1/2 tsp salt and pulse to combine (chickpeas should be chopped but coarse). Form mixture into twenty-four 2-tablespoon balls.
2. Heat air fryer to 325°F. Brush insert of basket with oil and add 12 falafel. Air-fry 15 minutes. Brush falafel with 1 tablespoon oil and increase air fryer temperature to 400°F. Air-fry until deeply golden, 4 more minutes. Repeat with remaining falafel.
3. In large bowl, whisk together lemon juice and remaining 2 tablespoons olive oil. Add cucumbers and marinate, 5 minutes. Add remaining 6 cups baby kale, parsley, and mint leaves, scallion greens, and 1/2 tsp salt and toss. Top with falafel and dollop of yogurt.

Tuna Egg Salad

Servings: 1
Cooking Time: 15 Minutes

Ingredients:
- 2 hard boiled eggs
- 1 2.6 oz packet light tuna in water (I use less sodium)
- 1 tablespoon mayonnaise ((check labels for whole30))
- 2 tablespoons chopped red onion
- salt and pepper (to taste)

Directions:
1. Chop the eggs and add them to a bowl with the tuna, mayo and red onion.
2. Mix to combine and season with salt and pepper to taste.
3. Eat right out of the bowl with a spoon or piled on a piece of toast, in a wrap, over greens, etc.

Air Fryer Green Bean Casserole

Servings: 6
Cooking Time: 12 Minutes

Ingredients:
- 10.5 ounce Cream of Mushroom Soup
- 1/2 cup milk
- 4 cups cooked cut green beans
- 1/2 tsp salt
- 1/2 tsp black pepper
- 1 1/2 cups crispy fried onions

Directions:
1. In a medium bowl, combine the soup, milk, salt, and pepper.
2. Stir in the green beans and half of the fried onions.
3. Pour mixture into the baking dish and cook for 350 degrees F for 12 minutes, stirring halfway through the cooking time.
4. Once done, top the baking dish with the remaining fried onions, and cook for an additional 2-3 minutes.

Crispy Smashed Potatoes With Herb Aioli

Servings: 2-4

Ingredients:
- Herb Aioli:
- ½ cup light mayo
- 1 teaspoon light sour cream
- 1 tablespoon fresh parsley, chopped
- 1 tablespoon fresh basil, chiffonade
- 1 tablespoon fresh chives, chopped
- 1 tablespoon fresh dill, chopped
- 1 tablespoon lemon juice
- ¼ teaspoon lemon zest
- 2 teaspoons extra virgin olive oil
- Kosher salt and pepper, to taste
- Potatoes:
- 1½ pounds small creamer potatoes
- 3 tablespoons avocado oil
- ¼ teaspoon cayenne pepper
- ½ teaspoon garlic powder
- 1 tablespoon black pepper

- 2 teaspoons kosher salt, plus more for boiling water
- ¼ teaspoon smoked paprika (optional)
- Oil spray

Directions:
1. Mix all the ingredients for the herb aioli in a small bowl and set aside to chill in the refrigerator.
2. Place the potatoes in a medium pot filled with cold salted water.
3. Boil the potatoes until a knife easily pierces through without any resistance.
4. Strain the potatoes and let cool for easy handling.
5. Combine the potatoes, avocado oil, cayenne pepper, garlic powder, black pepper, salt, and smoked paprika in a small bowl. Toss to coat.
6. Smash the potatoes gently with the palm of your hands, crushing them only halfway so that they stay intact.
7. Coat the Smart Air Fryer basket lightly with oil spray.
8. Place the potatoes directly into the air fryer basket, without the crisper plate.
9. Select the Air Fry function, adjust temperature to 400°F and time to 15 minutes, then press Start/Pause.
10. Remove the potatoes when done.
11. Serve hot with a side of aioli.

Spicy Canned Salmon Salad Rice Bowl

Servings: 1
Cooking Time: 0 Minutes

Ingredients:
- 1 5-ounce can skinless wild pink or red salmon (in water drained)
- 1 tablespoons light mayonnaise
- 2 teaspoons sriracha sauce (plus more for topping)
- 2 scallions (white and greens separated)
- Pinch kosher salt
- 3/4 cup cooked brown rice (heated)
- ½ cup chopped cucumber (I use Persian cucumbers)
- Furikake or chopped nori and sesame seeds (for garnish)

Directions:
1. In a small bowl, combine the salmon, mayonnaise, sriracha, scallion whites and pinch of salt and mix well.
2. In the bowl you plan to serve in, add the rice.
3. Top it with the salmon salad, chopped cucumber, furikake and scallion greens plus more sriracha if desired.

Chicken Caprese Salad Recipe

Servings: 4
Cooking Time: 10 Minutes

Ingredients:
- FOR THE CHICKEN:
- 2 tbsp Balsamic vinegar
- 1 tbsp Olive oil
- 1/2 tsp Garlic powder
- 1 tsp Dried basil
- 1/2 tsp Dried oregano
- 1 tsp Sea salt
- 1/4 tsp Black pepper
- 4 8-oz Boneless skinless chicken breasts
- FOR THE SALAD:
- 5 cups Romaine lettuce (chopped)
- 1 cup Cherry tomatoes (halved)
- 1/2 cup Fresh mozzarella balls
- 1/4 cup Fresh basil (cut into ribbons)
- 1/4 cup Balsamic glaze

Directions:
1. In a large bowl, whisk together balsamic vinegar, olive oil, garlic powder, dried basil, dried oregano, sea salt, and black pepper. Add the chicken breasts and turn to coat in the marinade. Set aside to marinate for at least 10 minutes, or marinate in the fridge for up to 8 hours.
2. Cook chicken breasts in the air fryer like this or in the oven like this. (Use the ingredients above, and check these links for cook times

and temperatures based on your preferred method.)
3. Let the chicken rest for 5 minutes, then slice against the grain. Cover to keep warm.
4. Meanwhile, make the balsamic glaze like this.
5. In a large salad bowl, combine lettuce, tomatoes, mozzarella balls, and chicken.
6. Sprinkle the salad with basil leaves and drizzle with balsamic glaze.

Air Fryer Bacon-wrapped Stuffed Jalapenos

Servings: 6
Cooking Time: 14 Minutes

Ingredients:
- 12 Jalapenos
- 8 ounces of cream cheese, room temperature or slightly soft
- 1/2 cup shredded cheddar cheese
- 1/4 teaspoon garlic powder
- 1/8 teaspoon onion powder
- 12 slices of bacon, thinly cut
- salt and pepper to taste

Directions:
1. Cut the jalapenos in half, remove the stems, and remove the seeds and membranes. The more membrane you leave, the spicier the jalapenos will be.
2. Add cream cheese, shredded cheddar cheese, garlic powder, onion powder, salt, and pepper in a bowl. Mix to combine.
3. Using a small spoon, scoop the cream mixture into each jalapeno filling it just to the top.
4. Preheat air fryer to 350 degrees for about 3 minutes.
5. Cut each slice of bacon in half.
6. Wrap each jalapeno half in one piece of bacon.
7. Place the bacon-wrapped stuffed jalapenos in the air fryer in an even layer making sure they do not touch.
8. Air fry at 350 degrees for 14-16 minutes, until bacon is thoroughly cooked.
9. Enjoy immediately or refrigerate for up to 3 days, reheating before eating.

Grilled Peach & Burrata Salad

Servings: 4

Ingredients:
- 2 peaches, cut into ½-inch-thick wedges
- 4 tablespoons olive oil, divided
- Kosher salt, to taste
- 6 cups arugula
- 8 ounces burrata cheese, torn
- ¼ cup toasted hazelnuts, chopped
- ¼ cup fresh mint leaves, torn
- 2 tablespoons balsamic vinegar, for drizzling
- Flaky sea salt, for finishing
- Freshly ground black pepper, for finishing

Directions:
1. Place the crisper plate into the Smart Air Fryer basket.
2. Select the Preheat function, then press Start/Pause.
3. Place the peaches and 1½ tablespoons olive oil in a medium bowl and toss to coat. Season with salt to taste.
4. Place the peaches onto the preheated crisper plate.
5. Select the Veggies function, adjust time to 9 minutes, then press Start/Pause.
6. Shake the peaches halfway through cooking. The Shake Reminder will let you know when.
7. Remove the peaches when done.
8. Divide the arugula between 4 plates and top with equal portions of peaches, burrata cheese, hazelnuts, and mint.
9. Drizzle the remaining olive oil and balsamic vinegar over each salad, season with flaky sea salt and freshly ground black pepper, then serve.

Colcannon Croquettes

Servings: 12

Ingredients:
- 1½ pounds baby Yukon gold potatoes, boiled until soft
- 2½ teaspoons plus 1 teaspoon kosher salt, divided
- 1½ teaspoons freshly ground black pepper
- 4 tablespoons unsalted butter, melted
- ¾ cup heavy whipping cream, divided
- 1 large egg
- 1½ cups kale, chopped
- 4 garlic cloves, minced
- ⅔ cup all-purpose flour
- 2½ cups panko breadcrumbs
- Oil spray

Directions:
1. Mash the boiled potatoes until smooth in a large bowl.
2. Whisk 2½ teaspoons salt, pepper, melted butter, ¼ cup cream, and egg together in a separate small bowl.
3. Pour the cream and egg mixture into the potatoes and stir to combine.
4. Fold in the kale and garlic to the mashed potatoes until evenly distributed.
5. Set up a breading station with the flour in one bowl, the remaining ½ cup cream in a second bowl, and the panko breadcrumbs and remaining 1 teaspoon of salt in a third bowl.
6. Shape the potatoes into 12 golf ball-sized balls. Roll each ball in flour, dip in cream, and finally dredge in panko breadcrumbs.
7. Place the breaded croquettes on a clean plate or tray.
8. Freeze the croquettes for 2 hours.
9. Place the crisper plate into the Smart Air Fryer basket, then place the croquettes onto the crisper plate and spray all over with oil spray.
10. Select the Frozen function, adjust time to 10 minutes, then press Start/Pause.
11. Remove the croquettes when done and serve.

SANDWICHES & BURGERS RECIPES

Air-fryer Cheeseburger Spring Rolls

Servings: 20
Cooking Time: 30 Minutes

Ingredients:
- 500g Woolworths BBQ classic beef burgers
- 3 gherkins, finely chopped
- 3 tbs tomato sauce (save 1 tbs to serve)
- 2 tbs American mustard (save 1 tbs to serve)
- 1 cup shredded pizza cheese
- 300g frozen spring roll pastry, thawed
- 5ml olive oil cooking spray

Directions:
1. Preheat air fryer to 180°C.
2. Using hands, combine beef burgers, gherkins, sauce, mustard and cheese in a
3. large bowl.
4. Place 1 pastry sheet on bench with 1 corner pointing towards you. Place 1 slightly heaped tablespoonful of mince mixture in middle of pastry. Fold corner nearest to you over filling then roll up, folding in sides to enclose filling. Transfer to a tray and cover with a damp tea towel (see Tip). Repeat with remaining pastry sheets and mince mixture to make a total of 20 spring rolls.

Tip: Covering rolls with a damp tea towel prevents them drying out.

Spray air-fryer basket with oil. Place half of the spring rolls in basket and spray with oil. Cook for 15 minutes, turning halfway through cooking, or until golden and crisp. Repeat with remaining spring rolls. Serve spring rolls drizzled with extra tomato sauce and mustard.

Air Fryer Turkey Burgers

Servings: 4
Cooking Time: 15 Minutes

Ingredients:
- 1 pound lean ground turkey
- ½ cup dried breadcrumbs
- 1 large egg
- 1 tablespoon ketchup
- ½ tablespoon Worcestershire sauce
- 1 teaspoon seasoning salt
- Black pepper, to taste
- Hamburger buns
- Lettuce, tomato, onion, or your favorite burger toppings

Directions:
1. Place the ground turkey in a mixing bowl with the breadcrumbs, egg, ketchup, Worcestershire sauce, seasoning salt, and pepper.
2. Use a fork to mix the contents of the bowl together well, being sure not to overmix.
3. Shape into four ½-inch thick round patties and place them on a large plate. Chill the patties in the fridge for at least 30 minutes
4. Preheat an air fryer to 360 degrees F for 5 minutes. Spray the air fryer basket with cooking spray, then place the burgers in an even layer in the basket.
5. Air fry for 15 minutes, flipping halfway through until an internal temperature of 165 degrees F is reached.

Air Fryer Hamburgers

Servings: 4
Cooking Time: 10 Minutes

Ingredients:
- 1 ½ pounds lean ground beef
- 1 tablespoon Worcestershire sauce
- salt & pepper to taste
- ¼ cup barbecue sauce optional
- for serving
- 4 hamburger buns
- lettuce, tomatoes, pickles, onions

Directions:
1. Preheat air fryer to 400°F.
2. Combine beef, Worcestershire sauce, and salt and pepper. Gently mix to combine.
3. Divide the mixture into four ½" thick patties and place in the air fryer in a single layer. Use your thumb to place a small indent in the middle of the burger patty.

4. Brush the burgers with the barbecue sauce, if using.
5. Cook 5 minutes, flip burgers, and cook an additional 4-6 minutes or until the burgers reach 160°F.
6. notes
7. When mixing burgers, mix gently.
8. 1 tablespoon of grated onion can be added to the beef mixture for extra flavor.
9. Air fryers can vary, check the burgers early to ensure they don't overcook.
10. Cheese can be added during the last 1 minute of cooking time.
11. Keep leftover air fryer burgers in a covered container in the refrigerator for up to 5 days. Freeze them in zippered bags for up to 8 weeks.

Air Fryer Amazing Burgers

Servings: 4
Cooking Time: 12 Minutes

Ingredients:
- 1.25 lb. (567 g) ground beef
- 1 teaspoon (5 ml) garlic powder
- 1 Tablespoon (15 ml) Worcestershire , fish sauce, or soy sauce (fish sauce is our favorite)
- 1/2 teaspoon (2.5 ml) salt , or to taste
- Lots of black pepper
- oil spray , for coating
- BURGER ASSEMBLY:
- 4 Buns , + optional cheese, pickles, lettuce, onion, tomato, avocado, cooked bacon etc.
- EQUIPMENT
- Air Fryer
- Instant Read Thermometer (optional)

Directions:
1. Preheat the Air Fryer at 380°F/193°C for about 4-5 minutes.
2. In bowl, combine beef, garlic, garlic powder Worcestershire sauce (or sauce of choice), salt and pepper. Mix everything until just combined.
3. Divide and flatten into 4 patties about 4" wide (don't pack the patties too firmly or else you'll have a dense burger - form just enough so that the patty holds its shape). Spray both sides with oil and spray the air fryer basket. If you have a smaller air fryer, you'll might need to cook in two batches.
4. Air Fry at 380°F/193°C for about 8-12 minutes, flip after 6 minutes. Cook to your preference or until the internal temperature reaches 160°F/71°C. Timing will vary depending on thickness of patties and individual air fryer model.
5. For Cheeseburgers: add the slices of cheese on top of the cooked patties. Air fry at 380°F/193°C for about 30 seconds to 1 minute to melt the cheese.
6. For best juiciness, cover the patties and let rest for about 3 minutes. While patties are resting, warm the buns in the air fryer at 380°F/193°C for about 1 minute. Serve on buns, topped with your favorite burger toppings.

Air Fryer Club Sandwich

Servings: 2
Cooking Time: 20 Minutes

Ingredients:
- 3 slice/s thick sandwich bread (we used Toastie bread)
- 6 rasher/s smoked streaky bacon
- 2 medium vine tomatoes
- 6 tsp Essential Mayonnaise
- 1/2 x 1 iceberg lettuce
- 150g leftover cooked turkey or chicken, thinly sliced
- 4 slice/s Emmental cheese
- salted crisps, to serve (optional)

Directions:
1. Toast the bread until golden brown (you can do this in the air fryer: put the bread on top of the rack and cook at 200°C for 4-6 minutes, turning every minute or so). Meanwhile, lay the bacon rashers on top of the rack in the basket of the air fryer and air-fry at 200°C for 6-8 minutes, turning them halfway, until very crisp.
2. Slice each tomato into 4-5 slices and season (snack on the ends – chef's treat). Spread

each slice of toast with 2 tsp mayonnaise. Tear the iceberg so you have 6-8 pieces about the same size as the bread. Divide the ingredients over 2 slices of toast, layering lettuce, then tomatoes, sliced chicken, bacon and cheese. Put one dressed slice on top of the other and close the sandwich with the empty slice, mayo-side down.

3. Insert 4 toothpicks into the sandwich. Slice with a bread knife into 4 triangles and serve immediately with crisps, if liked.

Cook's tip
If you don't have leftovers to hand, use a rolling pin to flatten 4 medium chicken breasts (150g each) between baking parchment, until they are of even thickness. Season, drizzle with 1 tbsp oil and air-fry at 180°C for 15-18 minutes, until cooked through, the juices run clear and there is no pink meat; you can check with a meat thermometer (75°C). Leave to rest for 10 minutes.

Customer safety tips
Follow manufacturer's instructions and advice for specific foods
Pre-heat the air fryer to the correct temperature
If cooking different foods together, be aware that they may require different times and temperatures
Spread food evenly – do not overcrowd pan/chamber
Turn food midway through cooking
Check food is piping/steaming hot and cooked all the way through
Aim for golden colouring – do not overcook

Turkey Burgers
Servings: 4
Cooking Time: 20 Minutes

Ingredients:
- 450g turkey mince
- 4 x spring onions
- 70ml Greek yoghurt
- 100g fresh breadcrumbs – made from 2 slices village bakery sliced bread
- Sae salt and black pepper
- 1 x pack 4 Burger buns
- Tomato, lettuce, red onion, cucumber and mayonnaise to serve

Directions:
1. Divide the mixture into 4 and roll into balls.
2. Flatten into burger shapes – put into the fridge to set for 10 mins.
3. Pre heat the airfryer to 180°C.
4. Put the burgers onto the fry tray – don't overlap.
5. Close the fry basket and cook for 20 mins.
6. Meanwhile toast the cut sides of the burger buns.
7. Spread some mayo on the bases – then some slices tomato, lettuce leaves, red onion and cucumber.
8. Top with a burger, then the bread top and serve.

Air Fryer Cheeseburger Bombs
Servings: 8
Cooking Time: 5 Minutes

Ingredients:
- 8 ounces crescent roll dough
- 1 1/2 pounds hamburger meat
- 1 1/2 cups cheddar cheese

Directions:
1. Preheat the Air Fryer to 400 degrees Fahrenheit.
2. Create meatballs with hamburger meat and cook at 400 degrees Fahrenheit for 10-12 minutes, depending on your preferred doneness.
3. Allow meatballs to cool for a few minutes after air frying.
4. Lay out each crescent roll sheet. Add cheese to the top of each dough sheet.
5. Top the cheese with a meatball, and then pinch the dough closed and use your hands to round them into little balls.
6. Place the cheeseburger balls into the basket of the air fryer and cook at 350 degrees Fahrenheit for 5 minutes.
7. Carefully remove cheeseburger bombs and dip into your favorite sauces such as mustard, ketchup, or BBQ sauce.

NOTES
This recipe was made with a 1700 watt 5.8 qt Cosori air fryer. All air fryers cook a little differently. You may need to adjust the cooking time based on your specific brand of air fryer.
You can use premade fresh or frozen meatballs to make this dish. Just add a little cooking time to the meatballs if you are making them from frozen.
You can change this recipe in several different ways. Consider seasoning the meatballs with your favorite burger seasoning, or simple things such as onion powder, salt, and pepper.
You can add additional items to the homemade meatballs or just to the burger bombs themselves. Consider adding items such as diced jalapenos, diced onions, or even small pieces of bacon.

Lentil Veggie Burger Recipe

Servings: 6
Cooking Time: 35 Minutes

Ingredients:
- Patties
- 3/4 cup (150 g) dry red lentils
- 1/2 cup (90 g) dry quinoa
- 2 cups (480 ml) vegetable broth
- 3 Tbsp ground chia seeds + 1/4 cup water
- 1/2 cup (60 g) pumpkin seeds (or nuts/seeds of choice)
- 2/3 cup (55 g) quick oats (gluten-free if needed)
- 1 Tbsp tomato paste
- 1 1/2 Tbsp tamari or coconut aminos
- 1 small onion chopped
- 3 garlic cloves chopped
- 2 tsp smoked paprika
- 1 tsp ground cumin
- 3/4 tsp sea salt or less/more to taste
- Black pepper to taste
- Other Ingredients:
- 2 Tbsp oil for frying
- Vegan BBQ sauce optional
- 6 burger buns regular or gluten-free
- Fresh veggies of choice e.g. tomatoes, lettuce, onion, cucumber
- Burger sauce

Directions:
1. You can watch the video in the post for visual instructions.
2. First, add the quinoa, red lentils, and veggie broth to a saucepan and bring it to a boil over high heat. Then, reduce the heat and simmer for about 15 minutes, or until the liquid absorbs. Increase the heat for a minute or two to evaporate all remaining liquid.
3. Meanwhile, mix three tablespoons of ground chia seeds with ¼ cup of water and set it aside to thicken. If you don't have ground chia seeds, blend the seeds for a few seconds in a blender or coffee/spice grinder.
4. Next, process the oats and pumpkin seeds in a food processor/blender for a few seconds. Then, add all the remaining ingredients to the processor, including the chia mixture, cooked quinoa, and lentils, and pulse again into a slightly chunky burger dough.
5. Be careful not to over-process the mixture into a paste, as the burgers should have some texture. If the mixture is too sticky, add some more oats. If it's too dry, add a little water.
6. Divide and shape the mixture into 6 burger patties with your hands.
7. Heat the oil in a large frying pan/ skillet (for alternative cooking methods, check the FAQs). Once hot, add three burger patties (or how many your pan will fit while not touching and easily able to flip) and cook for around 10 minutes, flipping halfway, until the burgers are firm and lightly crisp.
8. Repeat this with the remaining burgers.
9. Assemble the vegan hamburger with the salad veggies of your choice. Enjoy with a side of wedges and a salad.

Notes
Adjust the size: You can divide the mixture into smaller style 'fritters' or even smaller 'nuggets' with this same quinoa lentil burger mixture.
Cooking time may vary: Especially if you change the size of the patties.

For even-sized burgers: Divide the quinoa lentil mixture by weight (each weighing about 135-140 grams).

Store: Allow the cooked lentil patties to cool, and store any leftovers in an airtight container in the fridge for up to 5 days.

Frozen Hamburgers In The Air Fryer

Servings: 4
Cooking Time: 15 Minutes

Ingredients:
- 4 frozen hamburgers (1/4 to 1/2 pounds each)
- OPTIONAL (FOR SERVING)
- Hamburger buns
- Cheese
- Lettuce
- Tomato

Directions:
1. Preheat your air fryer to 370 degrees.
2. Place the frozen hamburgers in the air fryer and cook for 10 to 20 minutes, depending on cook preference (15 to 17 minutes for medium).
3. (optional) Turn your air fryer off and place a piece of cheese on each burger. Close your air fryer and let the cheese melt with the residual heat.
4. Remove the hamburgers from the air fryer and enjoy!

NOTES
Rare (125 degrees): approximately 13 minutes
Medium Rare (135 degrees): approximately 14 to 16 minutes
Medium (145 degrees): approximately 15 to 17 minutes
Medium Well (155 degrees): approximately 16 to 18 minutes
Well Done (160 degrees): approximately 17 to 20 minutes

Air Fryer Frozen Turkey Burgers

Servings: 4
Cooking Time: 18 Minutes

Ingredients:
- 4 frozen raw turkey patties, usually sold as either 1/4 lb.(113g) or 1/3 lb.(150g)
- salt, to taste if needed
- Lots of black pepper
- oil spray, for coating
- BURGER ASSEMBLY:
- 4 Buns, + optional cheese, pickles, lettuce, onion, tomato, avocado, cooked bacon etc.
- EQUIPMENT
- Air Fryer
- Instant Read Thermometer (optional)

Directions:
1. Spray both sides of frozen turkey patties with oil. Season with optional salt and pepper. Spray the air fryer basket with oil. Place the patties in the basket in a single layer. Cook in batches if needed.
2. 1/4 lb. frozen turkey patties: Air Fry at 380°F/193°C for a total of about 12-17 minutes. After the first 10 minutes flip the patties and continue Air Frying at 380°F/193°C for another 2-7 minutes or until it's cooked to your preferred doneness. The internal temperature should be 165°F/74°C.
3. 1/3 lb. frozen turkey patties: Air Fry at 380°F/193°C for a total of about 13-18 minutes. After the first 10 minutes flip the patties and continue Air Frying at 380°F/193°C for another 3-8 minutes or until it's cooked to your preferred doneness. The internal temperature should be 165°F/74°C.
4. Cheeseburgers: add the slices of cheese on top of the cooked patties. Air fry at 380°F/193°C for about 30 seconds to 1 minute to melt the cheese.
5. Cover the patties and let rest for 3 minutes. Warm the buns in the air fryer at 380°F/193°C for about 3 minutes while patties are resting. Serve on buns, topped with your favorite burger toppings.

VEGETABLE & & VEGETARIAN RECIPES

Crispy Air Fryer Roasted Brussels Sprouts With Balsamic

Servings: 4
Cooking Time: 15 Minutes

Ingredients:
- 1 pound brussels sprouts , ends removed and cut into bite sized pieces
- 2 Tablespoons olive oil , or more if needed
- 1 Tablespoon balsamic vinegar
- kosher salt , to taste
- black pepper , to taste

Directions:
1. Put cut brussels sprouts to bowl. Drizzle oil and balsamic vinegar evenly over the brussels sprouts. Don't dump the oil and vinegar in one spot or else it will just coat one brussels sprout. You want to make sure to coat all the brussels sprouts.
2. Sprinkle salt and pepper evenly over the brussels sprouts. Stir to combine everything and long enough so that all the brussels sprouts soaks up the marinade. There shouldn't be any marinade left in the bottom of the bowl.
3. Add brussels to the air fryer basket. Air fry at 360°F for about 15-20 minutes. Shake and gently stir half way through, about 8 minutes into cooking. Make sure you shake at the halfway mark! You don't wany to end up with uneven cooking. If needed, shake and toss a 3rd time to make sure it all cooks evenly.
4. Continue to air fry the brussels for the remainder of the time, or until the brussels are golden brown and cooked through. You can check earlier if needed to make sure nothing burns. Or you can add more time if needed to make sure it's cooked through.
5. Add additional salt and pepper if needed on the brussels sprouts and enjoy!

NOTES

Don't crowd the basket. If needed, it's better to cook in multiple smaller batches for even cooking, than it is to cook in one large batch. If cooking in multiple batches, the first batch will take longer to cook if Air Fryer is not already pre-heated.

If you decide to double the recipe, it will work great but make sure your air fryer is large enough (this recipe was cooked in a 3.7 qt air fryer). You might need add an additional 1-2 minutes of cooking time and give an extra shake or two while cooking if the basket is fairly full. Remember to set a timer to shake/flip/toss the food as directed in recipe.

Air Fryer Primavera Roasted Vegetables

Servings: 2-4

Ingredients:
- 1 small summer squash, trimmed and sliced into 1/4"-thick rounds
- 1 small zucchini, trimmed and sliced into 1/4"-thick rounds
- 1 small red bell pepper, stemmed, seeded, and cut into 1" pieces
- 2 tsp. extra-virgin olive oil
- 1 tsp. finely chopped fresh rosemary
- 1/4 tsp. kosher salt
- 1/4 tsp. freshly ground black pepper
- 1/4 c. grated Parmesan, plus more for serving
- Chopped fresh parsley, for serving

Directions:
1. In a large bowl, toss squash, zucchini, bell pepper, oil, rosemary, salt, and black pepper. Scrape vegetable mixture into an air-fryer basket; reserve bowl. Cook at 400° until vegetables are tender and golden in spots, about 12 minutes.

2. Return vegetables to reserved bowl and toss with Parmesan.
3. Divide vegetables among plates. Top with parsley and more Parmesan.

Air Fryer Onion Rings

Servings: 2-4
Cooking Time: 10 Minutes

Ingredients:
- 1/2 cup all-purpose flour
- 2 large eggs
- 1 1/4 cups panko bread crumbs
- 1 teaspoon chili powder optional
- 1/2 teaspoon garlic powder
- 1/2 teaspoon kosher salt plus additional for serving
- 1/8 teaspoon cayenne pepper optional
- 1 medium yellow onion sliced crosswise into 1/2- to 3/4-inch rings
- Nonstick cooking spray or olive oil
- Homemade BBQ Sauce for dipping (optional)

Directions:
1. In a small, shallow bowl, place the flour. In a second small bowl, beat the eggs. In a third bowl, combine the bread crumbs, chili powder, garlic powder, ½ teaspoon kosher salt, and cayenne. Last, line a baking sheet with parchment paper and keep it handy to use as a work surface.
2. Separate the onion slices into rings. Working a few at a time, dip the onion rings in the flour, then the eggs, then the bread crumb mixture, turning the rings and patting the panko as needed to adhere (smaller rings are easier than larger ones).
3. Place on the prepared baking sheet. Repeat with remaining rings.
4. Preheat your air fryer to 360 degrees F. Coat the air fryer basket with nonstick spray.
5. Place the onion rings in a single layer in the basket, then mist the tops with more nonstick spray.
6. Air fry the onion rings for 7 to 9 minutes, until golden and crisp (no need to flip them). Remove from the basket to a serving plate and immediately season with a pinch of salt. Repeat with the remaining onions. If you'd like to serve all batches hot at once, set the air fried rings aside as they finish, then reheat them all together in a single batch in the air fryer for a minute or two (it's OK to stack when reheating). Enjoy hot with BBQ sauce or dip of choice.

Notes
TO STORE: Refrigerate onion rings in an airtight storage container for up to 3 days.
TO REHEAT: Recrisp leftovers on a baking sheet in the oven at 350 degrees F.
TO FREEZE: Lay leftovers in a single layer on a baking sheet, then freeze until solid. Transfer the frozen rings to an airtight, freezer-safe storage container or ziptop bag. Freeze for up to 3 months. Reheat from frozen.

Cheesy Vegetarian 'sausage' Rolls

Servings: 16
Cooking Time: 20 Minutes

Ingredients:
- 1 tbsp olive oil
- 1 brown onion, finely chopped
- 2 garlic cloves
- 2 tsp Vegemite
- Pinch dried chilli flakes (optional)
- 200g button mushrooms, coarsely chopped
- 125g (1 cup) grated sweet potato
- 400g can brown lentils, rinsed, drained
- 2 tsp fresh thyme leaves
- 150g Devondale Colby Cheese Block (500g), cut into 1cm pieces
- 2 sheets frozen puff pastry, just thawed
- 1 egg, lightly whisked
- Tomato relish or tomato sauce, to serve
- Select all Ingredients:

Directions:
1. Preheat oven to 200C/180C fan forced. Line 2 baking trays with baking paper.

2. Heat the oil in a large frying pan over medium heat. Add the onion. Cook, stirring often, for 4-5 minutes or until soft. Add the garlic, Vegemite and chilli (if using) and cook, stirring, for 30 seconds or until aromatic. Add the mushroom and cook, stirring often, for 5 minutes or until soft and the liquid has evaporated. Add the sweet potato and cook, stirring, for 2 minutes or until softened. Stir in the lentils and thyme. Season. Transfer to a large heatproof bowl. Set aside, stirring often, for 15 minutes to cool. Stir in the cheese.
3. Cut each pastry sheet in half. Place one quarter of the sweet potato mixture in a log shape along one long edge of the pastry. Brush the opposite edge with egg. Roll up tightly to enclose. Repeat with the remaining pastry and filling. Cut each roll into 4 pieces and place, seam-side down, on the prepared trays.
4. Brush the pastry with egg and use a sharp knife to score lines into the top of the pastry. Bake for 25 minutes or until golden brown. Serve with tomato relish or sauce.

Air Fryer Broccoli And Carrots
Servings: 2
Cooking Time: 10 Minutes

Ingredients:
- 1 head broccoli rinsed
- 12 ounces carrots washed and peeled
- 2 Tablespoons olive oil
- 2 cloves garlic minced
- 1 teaspoon kosher salt
- 1/2 teaspoon ground black pepper

Directions:
1. Cut, peel, and wash carrots into ½-inch angled slices.
2. Cut the head of the broccoli into bite-sized florets.
3. Add broccoli and carrots into a large mixing bowl.
4. Add in the tablespoons of olive oil/avocado oil, minced garlic, salt, and black pepper. Mix together till the broccoli and carrots are coated.
5. Transfer the seasoned vegetables to the air fryer basket and cook at 390F for 10 minutes flipping halfway through. You will have to do these in batches. Also make sure the carrots are in a single layer and not stacked on top of each other.
6. Remove from the air fryer basket and serve.

NOTES
If you don't have regular carrots, baby carrots can be substituted. Make sure to cut them in half at a diagonal.
If I'm running short on time, I love to prep veggies earlier in the day and save them until I make the meal.

Air Fryer Baked Potatoes
Servings: 4
Cooking Time: 55 Minutes

Ingredients:
- 4 medium russet potatoes
- 1 tablespoon olive oil
- ½ teaspoon salt or to taste

Directions:
1. Scrub potatoes and towel dry. Poke each potato with a fork several times.
2. Rub the outside of the potato with oil and season with salt.
3. Place in the air fryer at 390°F and cook for 25 minutes. Flip the potatoes and cook for an additional 20-30 minutes or until tender when pierced with a fork.
4. Serve with desired toppings.

Air Fryer Roasted Potatoes Recipe
Servings: 4
Cooking Time: 20 Minutes

Ingredients:
- 1 pound baby Yukon Gold potatoes (about 1-inch wide)
- 1 tablespoon olive oil
- 2 teaspoons Italian seasoning

- 1/2 teaspoon garlic powder
- 1/2 teaspoon kosher salt
- 1/4 teaspoon freshly ground black pepper

Directions:
1. Heat an air fryer to 400°F. Meanwhile, halve 1 pound baby Yukon Gold potatoes and place in a medium bowl. Add 1 tablespoon olive oil, 2 teaspoons Italian seasoning, 1/2 teaspoon garlic powder, 1/2 teaspoon kosher salt, and 1/4 teaspoon black pepper, and toss to coat.
2. Arrange the potatoes in an even layer in the air fryer basket or tray (air fry in batches if needed). Air fry until lightly browned with crispy edges, tossing halfway through, about 20 minutes total.

NOTES
Storage: Refrigerate in an airtight container for up to 4 days.

Vortex Stuffed Mushrooms
Servings: 4
Cooking Time: 8 Minutes

Ingredients:
- Stuffing 1:
- 5 black mushrooms
- 2 Tbsp Butter
- 1 Tbsp Olive oil
- 1 Onion chopped
- 2 cloves garlic crushed
- 1 tsp Mixed herbs
- 1 Tbsp Fresh parsley chopped
- ¼ cup Grated cheddar or parmesan
- 30 ml Breadcrumbs
- Stuffing 2:
- 4 Black mushrooms
- 2 Tbsp Butter
- 1 Tbls olive oil
- ½ onion chopped
- 1 clove garlic
- 3 cups Baby spinach chopped
- Salt & pepper
- ¼ cup Feta

Directions:
1. Remove the stalks from 4 of the mushrooms.
2. Chop the stalks & remaining mushroom.
3. Top each mushroom with 1 tsp of butter.
4. Heat the remaining butter in a pan/Instant Pot on Saute with the olive oil.
5. Sauté the onion, garlic & mixed herbs until soft.
6. Add the chopped mushroom cook until mushroom is tender.
7. Add the fresh parsley.
8. Top each mushroom with the cooked mushroom mixture.
9. Top the grated cheese then breadcrumbs.
10. Place in the Vortex tray.
11. Set the Vortex to bake at 180C for 8 mins.
12. Place 1 tsp of butter on each mushroom.
13. In a pan/Instant Pot on Saute heat the remaining butter with the olive oil.
14. Sauté the onion & garlic until soft.
15. Add the spinach and stir until spinach has wilted.
16. Remove from heat & pour off excess liquid.
17. Season with salt & pepper.
18. Stir in the crumbled feta.
19. Top each mushroom with spinach mix.
20. Place in the Vortex tray.
21. Set the Vortex to bake at 180C for 8 mins.

Air Fryer Cauliflower With Garlic
Servings: 4
Cooking Time: 15 Minutes

Ingredients:
- 1 small head cauliflower (about 1.5 lbs./680g), cut into bite sized pieces
- 2 Tablespoons (30 ml) vegetable oil, or to taste
- 1/2 teaspoon (2.5 ml) garlic powder, or 3 cloves garlic minced
- 1/2 teaspoon (2.5 ml) kosher salt, or to taste
- 1/2 teaspoon (2.5 ml) black pepper, or to taste
- (optional) chopped parsley, for garnish

Directions:

1. Place the cut up cauliflower in a large bowl. In another bowl combine the oil, garlic powder (or minced garlic), salt, and pepper.
2. Alternate seasoning: Don't combine the seasonings. Instead, in the following step, just add the oil and individual seasonings to the caulifower. (Both ways work fine, some cooks like to combine everythign first, others don't want to dirty an extra bowl. You chose how you like to cook).
3. Pour about half of the seasoned marinade over the cauliflower. Toss and then repeat with the remaining seasonings (it helps season the cauliflower more evenly to mix in stages). Continue stirring the cauliflower until it completely soaks up all the marinade (there shouldn't be any marinade pooling at the bottom of the bowl).
4. Put the cauliflower into air fryer basket and spread evenly in the basket.
5. Air Fry at 360°F/180°C for 12-18 minutes, shake or gently turn half way. Cook to your desired tenderness and liking. Season with chopped parsely if desired.

Air Fryer Roasted Asparagus

Servings: 2
Cooking Time: 10 Minutes

Ingredients:
- 1 bunch fresh asparagus, trimmed
- avocado oil cooking spray
- ½ teaspoon garlic powder
- ½ teaspoon Himalayan pink salt
- ¼ teaspoon ground multi-colored peppercorns
- ¼ teaspoon red pepper flakes
- ¼ cup freshly grated Parmesan cheese

Directions:
1. Preheat the air fryer to 375 degrees F (190 degrees C). Line the basket with parchment paper.
2. Place asparagus spears in the prepared basket and mist with avocado oil. Sprinkle with garlic powder, salt, pepper, and pepper flakes. Top with Parmesan cheese.
3. Air-fry until asparagus spears start to char, 7 to 9 minutes.

Air Roasted Asparagus

Servings: 4
Cooking Time: 10 Minutes

Ingredients:
- 1 pound fresh asparagus , ends trimmed
- 1-2 teaspoons olive oil
- salt , to taste
- black pepper , to taste

Directions:
1. Wash and trim the tough ends of your asparagus. Coat asparagus with olive oil and season with salt and pepper. Add extra spices if you want. Make sure to coat the asparagus tips so they don't burn or dry out too fast.
2. Air Fry at 380°F for 7-10 minutes, depending on thickness, shake and turn asparagus halfway through cooking.
3. Let it cool a bit and taste for seasoning & tenderness. Cook for an extra minute or two if desired and season with extra salt and pepper if needed.

Crispy Air Fryer Brussels Sprouts

Servings: 4
Cooking Time: 11 Minutes

Ingredients:
- 1 lb brussels sprouts stem trimmed off and sliced in half; see note 1
- 1/4 cup water
- 1 tablespoon olive oil
- 1/4 teaspoon garlic powder
- 1/4 teaspoon onion powder
- 1/4 teaspoon salt

Directions:
1. Prepare brussels sprouts by trimming off the bottom ¼ inch of the stem and slicing in half.

2. Place brussels sprouts in a large microwave safe bowl, and add ¼ cup water. Cover and microwave for 3 minutes.
3. Carefully drain off the water, then toss the brussles sprouts in olive oil, garlic powder, onion powder and salt.
4. Heat air fryer to 200°F/390°F.
5. Add the brussels sprouts to the basket and cook for 7-8 minutes, shaking the basket every 3 minutes, or until the brussels sprouts are golden and crispy on the outside.
6. Serve.

Notes
Storage
After cooking, brussels sprouts may be stored in an air tight container in the fridge for up to 4 days.
Reheat
Heat the air fryer to 200°C/390°F. Add the brussels sprouts to the basket and cook for 3-4 minutes, until warmed through.
Variations
balsamic– add 1 tablespoon of balsamic vinegar to the oil and toss the brussels sprouts
OR drizzle with balsamic reduction for a sweet and tangy flavor booster
parmesan cheese– to serve, sprinkle with 2-4 tablespoons of freshly grated parmesan cheese
Asian-inspired– add 1 tablespoon of soy sauce to the oil when tossing and sprinkle with sesame seeds to serve
lemon garlic– add 4 cloves of crushed garlic and serve with fresh lemon wedges

Steamed Veggies

Servings: 2
Cooking Time: 10 Minutes

Ingredients:
- 1 cup cauliflower florets
- 1 cup broccoli florets
- ½ cup carrot, sliced into ¼-inch circles
- Cooked brown rice, for serving

Directions:
1. Fill the inner pot of the Rice Cooker with water until it reaches the steam line.
2. Place the vegetables into the steam basket, then place the steam basket into the rice cooker.
3. Set Mode to Steam, then tap Start. Check on the cauliflower and broccoli after 8 minutes if you like your vegetables crisper.
4. Remove the steam basket and transfer the vegetables to a bowl, then serve with brown rice.

Popcorn Vegan Pieces With Buffalo Sauce

Servings: 2

Ingredients:
- 1 pack Quorn Vegan Pieces
- 2 tsp smoked paprika
- 1 tsp brown sugar
- 1 tsp cornflour
- 1 tsp onion powder
- 1 tsp garlic powder
- 100ml Aquafaba (liquid from drained tin of chickpeas)
- 40g panko breadcrumbs
- 1 tbsp dried thyme
- 1/2 tsp salt
- For the Buffalo Sauce
- 1 tbsp maple sauce
- 1 tbsp sriracha chilli sauce
- 1 tbsp apple cider vinegar

Directions:
1. Preheat air fryer to 180C, we used the Ninja Foodi Dual Zone Air Fryer. Line a large baking tray or chopping board with baking paper
2. Combine the paprika, sugar, cornflour, onion powder and garlic powder in a medium shallow dish. Add the frozen Quorn Vegan Pieces, a few pieces at a time, and stir to coat. Transfer to the prepared tray
3. Drain the chickpeas and keep for another meal, reserve the chickpea water (aka

Aquafaba). Add the coated pieces, a few pieces at a time, and stir to coat. Return pieces to the tray
4. Combine the panko breadcrumbs and thyme in another medium shallow dish. Add the pieces, a few pieces a time, and turn to coat
5. Line your air fryer drawer with baking paper (use both drawer zones if using Ninja Foodi Dual Zone Air Fryer). Place crumbed pieces inside. Select Air Fry and set time to 10 minutes. Press Start/Stop to begin. Fry for 10 minutes or until the crust is golden
6. While the pieces are cooking, make the buffalo sauce by placing all ingredients into a small serving bowl and whisk to combine
7. Transfer the pieces onto a serving plate. Sprinkle with cracked black pepper & thyme and drizzle over a little buffalo sauce. Serve with remaining sauce

Instant Pot & Vortex Smashed Baby Potatoes

Servings: 4
Cooking Time: 16 Minutes

Ingredients:
- 500g Baby potatoes
- Salt & pepper
- Paprika
- 2 sprigs Thyme
- 2 Tbls Olive oil

Directions:
1. Rinse the baby potatoes and place in the Instant Pot with ½ cup water.
2. Pressure Cook on High Pressure for 5 mins.
3. Allow a Natural Presssure Release release for 5 mins then release the remaining pressure.
4. Remove the potatoes from the Instant Pot.
5. Place in the Vortex draw (or Duo Crisp) and gently squash each potato.
6. Drizzle with olive oil and season with salt, pepper, paprika & thyme.
7. Set the Vortex (or Duo Crisp) to Roast at 200C for 6 mins.

Mashed Potato Balls

Servings: 20
Cooking Time: 15 Minutes

Ingredients:
- 3 cups leftover mashed potatoes
- 1/2 cup cheddar cheese, shredded
- 1/4 cup green onions, finely chopped
- 1 teaspoon garlic powder
- 1/2 teaspoon paprika
- 1/2 teaspoon salt (or to taste)
- 1/4 teaspoon ground black pepper (or to taste)
- 2 cups panko breadcrumbs
- vegetable oil (for frying)

Directions:
1. In a large mixing bowl, add mashed potatoes, cheese, green onions, garlic powder, paprika, salt and pepper. Mix well until smooth.
2. Take 2 tablespoons of the potato mixture at a time and shape into balls by hand, similar to shaping meatballs. Alternatively, you can use a cookie scoop to shape into even pieces.
3. Add breadcrumbs in a large bowl. Dip the mashed potato balls in crumbs and gently press crumbs around each ball to coat.
4. Arrange the coated mashed potato balls evenly on a parchment-lined half sheet baking pan and transfer into the freezer. Freeze for 15-20 minutes to firm up. This helps the mashed potato bites hold their shape when deep-frying.
5. Add 2-inches of oil into a cooking pot and heat over medium-high heat until shimmering hot, about 3-4 minutes. Add the potato balls in batches (about 4-5 pieces each time) until crisp and golden brown, about 1-2 minutes. Turn the balls occasionally to get an even golden crust on all sides.

6. Transfer the potato balls to a paper towel lined plate to drain excess oil, and let them cool for 5 minutes before serving.

NOTES

How to cook in the air fryer: Preheat the air fryer to 375 F, about 3 minutes. Carefully place mashed potato in a single layer in the air fryer basket and lightly spray with cooking oil to coat evenly. Air fry the mashed potato bites for 10-15 minutes until golden brown. Gently shake the basket halfway during cooking to brown evenly.

How to freeze: I recommend freezing these mashed potato balls before you cook them. Prepare them up to the point of frying, then arrange the balls in a single layer on a large half sheet baking pan. Freeze until hard, about 1 hour. Then transfer to a freezer bag or airtight container and freeze for up to 3 months.

How to cook from frozen: Cook in the same way that you would when following the recipe. It will take a few minutes longer to cook until crisp and golden brown.

How to store: Make sure the fried mashed potato balls cool to room temperature completely before storing. Skipping this step can result in soggy potato bites. Then, transfer the balls to an airtight container and refrigerate for up to 4-5 days.

How to reheat: Reheat leftover mashed potato balls in a 375F oven for 15-20 minutes, or air fryer for 10 minutes.

Make ahead instructions: If you want to prep these mashed potato balls ahead of time, make them the day or morning before and store them in the freezer. Then, when it's time to serve, quickly fry them up. You could also cook them in advance, refrigerate, and pop into the oven to reheat.

Air Fryer Baby Carrots

Servings: 6
Cooking Time: 15 Minutes

Ingredients:
- 1 pound baby carrots
- 1 tablespoon olive oil
- 1 teaspoon italian seasoning
- ½ teaspoon salt
- ¼ teaspoon pepper
- Fresh parsley for garnish, optional

Directions:
1. Preheat your air fryer to 370 F.
2. In a medium bowl, toss the baby carrots with the oil and seasonings until everything is uniformly coated.
3. Transfer carrots to the air fryer basket and cook for 12-15 minutes, shaking the basket halfway through, or until tender all the way through.
4. Garnish with parsley and serve warm.

Air Fryer Veggie Chip Medley

Servings: 4

Ingredients:
- Deselect All
- 1 sweet potato (about 4 ounces), scrubbed
- 1 purple potato (about 4 ounces), scrubbed
- 2 tablespoons olive oil
- Kosher salt and freshly ground black pepper
- 1 red beet (about 6 ounces), scrubbed
- 1 golden beet (about 6 ounces), scrubbed

Directions:
1. Thinly slice both potatoes on a mandoline, about 1/16 inch thick. Transfer to a medium bowl and run under cold water until almost all the white starch comes off and the water runs clear. Dry well between a few paper towels. Dry the bowl as well.
2. Return the dry potatoes back to the bowl and toss with 1 tablespoon of the oil, 1/2 teaspoon salt and a few grinds of pepper until evenly coated.
3. Preheat a 5-quart air fryer to 320 degrees F. Shingle the potatoes in the bottom of the basket; it's okay if there are two layers. Cook until the potatoes are golden around the edges and crisp, tossing every 5 minutes with tongs so they're evenly cooked, 20 to 25 minutes. If you notice a few slices are finished cooking and completely crisp

before others, remove to a bowl and continue air frying the remaining pieces.
4. Meanwhile, thinly slice both beets on the mandoline, about 1/16 inch thick. Transfer to another medium bowl and toss with the remaining 1 tablespoon oil, 1/2 teaspoon salt and a few grinds of pepper until evenly coated.
5. Return the air fryer to 320 degrees F. Shingle the beets in the bottom of the basket; it's okay if there are two layers. Cook until the beets are darkened around the edges and crisp, tossing every 5 minutes so they're evenly cooked, about 30 minutes. If you notice a few slices are finished cooking and completely crisp before others, remove to a bowl and continue air frying the remaining pieces.
6. Combine the beet chips and potato chips in a large bowl, season with a pinch of salt and toss to combine. Serve immediately or let cool and store in an airtight container for up to 2 days.

Air Fryer Baked Potato
Servings: 3
Cooking Time: 35 Minutes

Ingredients:
- 3 medium Russet potatoes (washed and dried)
- 1 tbsp Olive oil
- 1/2 tsp Sea salt
- 1 1/2 tbsp Butter (for topping)

Directions:
1. Preheat the air fryer to 400 degrees F (204 degrees C) for about 5 minutes.
2. Prick the potatoes all over with a knife or fork.
3. Drizzle the potatoes with oil and rub in, or brush the oil on with a brush. Sprinkle with sea salt.
4. Place the potatoes in the air fryer basket in a single layer. Make sure there is space between them to allow the skins to crisp up nicely.
5. Bake potatoes in the air fryer for 35-45 minutes, turning halfway through with tongs. (Cook time can vary depending on the size of the potatoes.) They are done when a fork pierced into the potatoes goes in easily.
6. When done, move potatoes to bowls and cool slightly. Slice lengthwise down the middle, fluff with a fork, and top each potato with ½ tablespoon of butter. See the post above for more topping ideas.

Air Fryer Grilled Tomato And Cheese
Servings: 2
Cooking Time: 9 Minutes

Ingredients:
- 4 slices sourdough bread
- 4 slices tomato
- 1 cup Gruyere cheese shredded
- 1 teaspoon basalmic vinegar
- 1 Tablespoon unsalted butter melted

Directions:
1. Spread a light coat of butter onto both sides of each slice of bread.
2. Assemble each sandwich by adding slices of tomato, ½ cup shredded Gruyere cheese, and then brushing the tomatoes with the balsamic vinegar.
3. Place prepared sandwiches in a single layer into the basket of the air fryer.
4. Air fry the tomato and cheese sandwiches at 370 degrees Fahrenheit for 8-10 minutes, flipping halfway through. Remove from the air fryer when they've reached your preferred level of golden, crispy brown.

NOTES
This recipe was made in the 1700 watt 5.8 quart basket style Cosori air fryer. If you are using a different size or different brand of air fryer, you may need to adjust the cooking time slightly. All air fryers will cook a little differently.
Consider using different cheeses such as American, Provolone, or Swiss cheese to change the flavors.

Easy Air Fryer Baked Potatoes

Servings: 4
Cooking Time: 40 Minutes

Ingredients:
- 4 large baking potatoes, scrubbed
- 2 tablespoons olive oil
- kosher salt and freshly ground black pepper to taste
- ½ teaspoon garlic powder, or to taste
- ½ teaspoon dried parsley, or to taste
- 4 tablespoons butter

Directions:
1. Preheat an air fryer to 400 degrees F (200 degrees C).
2. Rub potatoes with olive oil and season with salt, pepper, garlic powder, and parsley. Place potatoes in the air fryer basket.
3. Cook in the preheated air fryer until potatoes are soft, 40 to 50 minutes, depending on potato size.
4. Slice potatoes lengthwise. Pinch both sides of each potato, using your hands and forcing potatoes to open, until the fluffy insides start to come out. Add 1 tablespoon of butter into each potato.

Cauliflower Buffalo Bites With Ranch Dressing

Servings: 4

Ingredients:
- 150g gram flour
- 1 tsp onion powder
- 1 tsp garlic powder
- 1 tsp ground cumin
- 1 tsp paprika
- salt, as desired
- ground black pepper, as desired
- 250ml unsweetened plant-based milk
- 700g cauliflower, cut into 5cm florets
- cooking spray
- 30ml sunflower oil
- 70ml buffalo sauce
- Ranch Dressing
- 100ml egg free mayonnaise
- 50ml unsweetened plant-based milk
- 1 tbsp fresh chopped parsley
- 1 tbsp fresh chopped chives
- 1 tsp garlic powder
- 1 tsp onion powder

Directions:
1. In a large bowl, add gram flour, onion powder, garlic powder, cumin, paprika, salt and pepper. Gradually whisk in milk until a smooth batter is formed.
2. Dip cauliflower florets into batter to evenly coat.
3. Insert crisper plates in both zone drawers, then spray the crisper plate with oil. Arrange cauliflower in an even layer in both drawers.
4. Select zone 1, turn the dial to select AIR FRY, set temperature to 170c, and set time to 15 minutes. Select MATCH. Press the dial to begin cooking.
5. While cauliflower cooks, prepare the buffalo sauce. In a small bowl, whisk the oil and buffalo sauce together.
6. Reinsert the baskets in the unit. Select zone 1, turn the dial to select AIR FRY, set temperature to 170c, and set time to 12 minutes. Select MATCH. Press the dial to begin cooking.
7. While cauliflower cooks, prepare the ranch dressing. In a small bowl, which all the dressing ingredient together until smooth.
8. When cooking is complete, serve the buffalo cauliflower bites with ranch dressing.

Garlic Mashed Potatoes

Servings: 4-6
Cooking Time: 40 Minutes

Ingredients:
- 1 head garlic, whole and unpeeled
- 1 tablespoon extra virgin olive oil
- 2 pounds potatoes, preferably Yukon Gold or another yellow, waxy potato
- 1/2 teaspoon salt, plus more to taste
- 1/3 cup cream
- 3 tablespoons butter

Directions:
1. Preheat the oven:
2. Preheat the oven to 400°F.
3. Roast the garlic:
4. Remove the outer layer of papery skin of the whole garlic head, leaving the head itself intact.
5. Using a paring knife, slice off the tops (1/4 to 1/2 inch) of the garlic cloves so they are all exposed. Place the garlic head on a piece of aluminum foil. Drizzle olive oil over the garlic head, salt lightly, and wrap the foil lightly around the garlic.
6. Bake at 400°F for 30 to 40 minutes, or until the cloves feel soft to the touch and are beginning to brown. Remove from the oven and let cool.
7. Boil the potatoes:
8. While the garlic is roasting, peel and chop the potatoes into 1-inch chunks. Place potatoes in a medium saucepan, add 1/2 teaspoon salt, cover with cold water.
9. Bring the pot to a boil, reduce to a simmer, and simmer potatoes until tender when pierced with a fork, about 15 minutes.
10. Warm the cream and melt the butter:
11. Either in a small pan on the stovetop or in a bowl in the microwave, combine the cream and butter. Cook over low heat until the butter is melted and the cream is warmed through.
12. Mash the potatoes with garlic:
13. Drain the pot with the potatoes and put it back on the stovetop over low heat. Put the drained potatoes back in the pot.
14. Squeeze the roasted garlic into the potatoes and begin mashing with a potato masher or a large fork.
15. Add the cream and butter, then season:
16. Add the cream and butter and mash until the potatoes are the consistency you want. Do not over-beat them, or the potatoes will become gummy.
17. Taste for salt and add some more, if needed.

Air Fryer Tofu
Servings: 4
Cooking Time: 10 Minutes

Ingredients:
- 15 oz tofu extra firm
- 1/2 tablespoon olive oil
- 1/2 tablespoon sesame oil
- 2 tablespoons soy sauce
- 1/2 teaspoon garlic powder
- 1/2 teaspoon ground ginger
- 1/4 teaspoon salt

Directions:
1. Preheat the air fryer to 190C/375F.
2. Cube the tofu into bite sizes pieces. Place the tofu on a dishtowel or paper towel to soak up excess moisture.
3. In a large bowl, combine the olive oil, sesame oil, soy sauce, garlic powder, and salt. Add the tofu and mix well, until all the tofu is coated.
4. Generously grease the air fryer basket and add a single layer of tofu to it. Air fry for 10-12 minutes, shaking the basket several times throughout.
5. Once the tofu is golden brown, remove it from the basket and repeat the process until all the tofu is cooked up.

Notes
TO STORE: Store leftover crispy tofu in an airtight container in the fridge for up to 4 days.
TO REHEAT: To reheat air-fried tofu, preheat the air fryer to 375F degrees. Add tofu to the air fryer basket and cook for a few minutes until heated through.
TO FREEZE: You can also freeze air-fried tofu if you have made a big batch. Flash-freeze tofu and transfer it into an airtight bag or container. Keep cooked tofu in the freezer for up to 3 months.

FAVORITE AIR FRYER RECIPES

Crispy Peanut Tofu With Squash Noodles
Servings: 4
Cooking Time: 20 Minutes

Ingredients:
- FOR THE PEANUT SAUCE:
- 6 tablespoons powdered peanut butter I like PB2
- 1 clove garlic small, finely grated
- 1/2 teaspoon ginger paste
- 1 tablespoon low-sodium tamari or low-sodium soy sauce
- 1 teaspoon toasted sesame oil
- 1/2 teaspoon Chinese cooking wine
- FOR THE PEANUT TOFU AND SQUASH NOODLES:
- 14 ounces extra firm tofu drained, pressed and diced into cubes
- 2 tablespoons low-sodium tamari or low-sodium soy sauce
- 1 teaspoon toasted sesame oil
- 1 tablespoon cornstarch
- 2 teaspoons toasted sesame seeds optional
- olive oil spray
- 2 medium yellow squash spiralized
- 2 medium zucchinis spiralized
- 6 to 8 ounces shiitake mushrooms stems removed and caps sliced
- 1/4 teaspoon garlic powder
- FOR SERVING:
- 1/4 cup chopped peanuts for serving
- cilantro chopped, for serving
- 2 green onions sliced, for serving
- sambal oelek for serving
- lime wedges for serving
- sesame seeds for serving

Directions:
1. FOR THE SAUCE:
2. In a small bowl, combine the powdered peanut butter with 3 tablespoons of water, mixing until combined.
3. Next stir in the garlic, ginger, tamari, toasted sesame oil and Chinese cooking wine.
4. When ready to serve, heat in a small sauce pan until warmed
5. FOR THE TOFU AND SQUASH NOODLES:
6. Cut the (pressed) tofu into ½-inch cubes.
7. In a medium bowl, combine 2 tablespoons tamari, 1 teaspoon sesame oil and cornstarch. Once combined, toss with sesame seeds.
8. Then, preheat your air fryer to 390° or 400° depending on your model. Working in batches, add the tofu in a single layer and air fry for 8 to 10 minutes or until crispy. Transfer to a paper towel lined plate and repeat with the remaining tofu.
9. Then add the sliced shiitake into the air fryer and cook for 4 minutes. You can reheat the tofu by adding it back into your air fryer and heating for a minute or two.
10. FOR THE SQUASH NOODLES:
11. Heat a 10-inch skillet over medium heat and spray with olive oil spray.
12. Once hot, add the spiralized squash noodles and the garlic powder. Toss occasionally until tender yet still a bit firm. About 7 to 8 minutes.
13. Finally serve the zoodles into bowls and add the crispy tofu, shiitake mushrooms and peanut sauce. Then top with crushed peanuts, sliced green onions, sesame seeds and minced cilantro. Don't forget about the wedge of lime on the side.

Mama Sue's Salsa

Ingredients:
- 28 oz. can diced tomatoes
- 3 stalks green onion, cut into thirds
- 10-12 stalks cilantro (leaves only), cut into thirds
- 1 jalapeno
- 1 lime, cut in half and juiced

- 1 tsp pepper
- 1 tsp seasoned salt
- 1 tsp coriander
- 1 tsp chili powder
- 1 tsp garlic salt

Directions:
1. Roughly chop the green onion and cilantro.
2. Slice your jalapeno in half. To change the level of heat in your salsa, then add or take away the seeds.
3. Cut your lime in half.
4. Drain half of the juice from the canned tomatoes and discard.
5. In your blender, add in the cilantro, green onions, jalapenos and remaining tomato juice. Squeeze in as much lime as desired. Place the lid on and pulse until chopped semi-finely.
6. Add in the diced tomatoes, spices and desired level of jalapeno seeds. *If you decide after you've added the jalapeno seeds, that you want a little more spice, then feel free to add chili pepper or paprika!
7. Pulse until you get your desired consistency. Serve at room temperature with your favorite tortilla chips. Enjoy!
8. *make homemade tortilla chips in an air fryer to go with salsa. They only need a couple minutes in the air fryer and you've got a crispy side to go along with it!

Air Fryer Pizza Recipe

Servings: 4-6
Cooking Time: 1 Hour 20 Minutes To 1 Hour 36 Minutes

Ingredients:
- 1 pound pizza dough, thawed if frozen
- Cooking spray
- 1 cup prepared pizza sauce
- 2 2/3 cups shredded Italian cheese blend
- TOPPING OPTIONS:
- Pepperoni
- Sliced mushrooms
- Sliced peppers

Directions:
1. Divide 1 pound pizza dough into 8 (2-ounce) pieces. If refrigerated, let sit on the counter until room temperature, at least 30 minutes.
2. Heat an air fryer to 375°F.
3. Press each piece of pizza dough into a round up to 6 1/2-inches wide, or 1/2 inch smaller than the size of your air fryer basket.
4. Coat the air fryer basket with cooking spray and carefully transfer one round of dough into the basket. (The basket will be warm.) Gently press the dough to the edges of the basket without touching the sides. Spread 2 tablespoons pizza sauce onto the dough, then sprinkle with 1/3 cup of the shredded cheese and top with any desired toppings.
5. Air fry until the crust is golden-brown and the cheese is melted, 10 to 12 minutes.
6. Carefully lift the pizza out of the air fryer basket with tongs or a spatula. Place on a cutting board and cut into wedges. Serve immediately and repeat with the remaining dough and toppings.

RECIPE NOTES
Storage: Leftovers can be refrigerated in an airtight container for up to 3 days.

Air Fryer Stuffed Jalapenos

Servings: 2
Cooking Time: 7 Minutes

Ingredients:
- 3 jalapenos cut in half lengthwise and deseeded
- ¼ cup cream cheese softened
- ¼ cup nacho cheese mix shredded
- 1 tablespoon bacon bits
- 1 green onion sliced

Directions:
1. Preheat the air fryer to 350°F.
2. Cut the jalapenos lengthwise and remove the seeds
3. In a small bowl combine the remaining ingredients and mix until combined.
4. Fill each jalapeno with the cheese mixture and place in the air fryer basket.

5. Cook jalapenos for 5-7 minutes or until the peppers are tender and cheese has browned on top.

Notes

If you want to cook larger amounts, simply double or triple. If you try to do more than one rack at a time, you will need to rotate them and make sure to not put any racks higher than the middle rung, they will get scorched on the top!

Salami Chips

Servings: 4

Ingredients:
- 1/2 lb. sliced salami, about ⅛-inch thick
- 1/2 c. mayonnaise
- 2 tbsp. red wine vinegar
- 1 tbsp. parsley, finely chopped
- 2 tsp. Dijon mustard
- 1 tsp. dried oregano
- kosher salt
- Freshly ground black pepper

Directions:
1. FOR OVEN
2. Preheat oven to 325° and line a medium baking sheet with parchment paper. Place salami in a single layer on baking sheet and bake until crisp, 20 to 25 minutes.
3. Meanwhile, make sauce: In a medium bowl, combine remaining ingredients. Whisk until smooth.
4. Serve salami chips with sauce on side.
5. FOR AIR FRYER
6. Working in batches, place salami in a single layer in basket of air fryer and bake at 375° for 6 minutes.
7. Meanwhile, make sauce: In a medium bowl, combine remaining ingredients. Whisk until smooth. Serve salami chips with sauce on side.

Frozen Potstickers In The Air Fryer

Servings: 2
Cooking Time: 10 Minutes

Ingredients:
- DUMPLINGS
- 8 ounces frozen vegetable, pork, or chicken dumplings
- DIPPING SAUCE
- 1/4 cup soy sauce
- 1/4 cup water
- 1/8 cup maple syrup (or molasses)
- 1/2 teaspoon garlic powder
- 1/2 teaspoon rice vinegar
- small pinch of red pepper flakes

Directions:
1. Preheat your air fryer to 370 degrees for about 4 minutes.
2. Place the frozen dumplings inside the air fryer in one layer and spray with oil.
3. Cook for 5 minutes, shake the basket, then spray with a little more oil.
4. Cook dumplings for another 4-6 minutes.
5. Meanwhile, prepare the dipping sauce by mixing ingredients together.
6. Remove the air fryer dumplings from the basket and let sit for another 2 minutes before enjoying.

Air-fryer Katsu Bites

Servings: 10
Cooking Time: 25 Minutes

Ingredients:
- 1/4 cup plain flour
- 1 tsp curry powder
- 2 free range eggs, lightly beaten
- 1 1/2 cups panko breadcrumbs
- 600g Woolworths RSCPA-approved chicken tenderloins
- 1 tsp sesame seeds, toasted
- 1/2 tsp poppy seeds
- 1/2 tsp cayenne pepper
- 1/4 bunch coriander, leaves picked
- 1/3 cup tonkatsu sauce

Directions:

1. Combine flour and curry powder on a plate. Season with pepper. Place egg and breadcrumb in separate shallow dishes.
2. Using one piece of chicken at a time, coat chicken in flour mixture, shaking off excess. Dip in egg, then roll in breadcrumbs to coat. Place on a baking tray lined with baking paper. Refrigerate for 10 minutes to let the crumb coat set.
3. Preheat air fryer to 180ºC for 2 minutes. Arrange half the chicken, in a single layer, in the air-fryer basket. Cook for 10-12 minutes or until golden and cooked through. Repeat with remaining chicken.
4. Combine sesame seeds, poppy seeds and cayenne pepper in a small bowl. Place chicken on a serving plate. Sprinkle with sesame mixture and coriander leaves.
5. Serve with sauce.

Pepperoni Pizza Bites

Servings: 4
Cooking Time: 30 Minutes

Ingredients:
- Olive oil spray
- 1 cup unbleached all-purpose flour (whole wheat or gluten-free mix, (5 oz in weight))
- 2 teaspoons baking powder (make sure it's not expired, or it won't rise)
- 3/4 teaspoon kosher salt (diamond crystal, use less if using table salt or Mortons)
- 1 cup non-fat Greek yogurt (not regular yogurt, it will be too sticky (I recommend Stonyfield))
- 2/3 cup marinara or pizza sauce
- 1 cup shredded part-skim mozzarella cheese
- 1 ounce turkey pepperoni (chopped)
- Crushed red pepper flakes (for serving (optional))

Directions:
1. Preheat oven to 375°F and spray two 12-cup stand size muffin tins with oil.
2. In a medium bowl combine the flour, baking powder and salt and whisk well.
3. Add the yogurt and mix with a fork or spatula until well combined, it will look like small crumbles.
4. Lightly dust flour on a work surface and remove dough from the bowl, knead the dough a few times until dough is tacky, but not sticky, about 15 turns (it should not leave dough on your hand when you pull away).
5. Divide the dough into 16 equal-size small balls (about 25 grams each).
6. Press each ball into the bottom of the muffin cups, allowing it to go up the side slightly.
7. Bake for 15 minutes, remove from oven and carefully press balls down in the middle to create a small well.
8. Top each ball with 2 teaspoons sauce, 1 tablespoon cheese and a sprinkle of pepperoni.
9. Return to the oven and bake 3 minutes, or until cheese is melted.
10. Remove from oven and allow to cool 2 minutes. With a paring knife or metal offset spatula, carefully remove the bites, cutting around the top to remove any cheese that may have stuck to the pan.
11. Spray the pan again and repeat with remaining dough and toppings.

Dutch Baby

Servings: 3

Ingredients:
- 3 extra-large eggs, room temperature
- ½ cup all-purpose flour, sifted
- ½ cup whole milk, room temperature
- 1 tablespoon granulated sugar
- 1 teaspoon ground nutmeg
- 2½ tablespoons unsalted butter
- ½ lemon, juiced, for sprinkling (optional)
- Confectioner's sugar, for dusting
- Fresh berries, for garnish (optional)
- Items Needed:
- 7-inch cast iron pan or 7-inch cake pan
- Metal sieve
- Oven mitt or kitchen towels

Directions:
1. Place the cast iron pan or cake pan into the Air Fryer basket.
2. Select the Preheat function on the air fryer, adjust temperature to 375°F, then press Start/Pause.
3. Whisk the eggs, flour, milk, sugar, and nutmeg in a large bowl until well combined and smooth. There should be no lumps.
4. Remove the air fryer basket after preheating, keeping the cast iron pan inside the basket. Immediately add in the butter and use a spatula to spread the butter around evenly until it has melted.
5. Pour the batter into the cast iron pan and reinsert the basket back into the air fryer.
6. Set temperature to 375°F and time to 20 minutes, then press Start/Pause. The pancake will puff up and grow in height, no shake is necessary but if you would like a lighter colored topping, pause the air fryer when 5 minutes is left on the timer and tent the top of the pancake with foil.
7. Remove the cast iron pan, carefully with an oven mitt, when done. Turn out the Dutch baby onto a serving platter and serve at once sprinkled with lemon juice, dusted with confectioner's sugar, and fresh berries if desired.

Air Fryer Churro Bites

Ingredients:
- 1 CUP water
- 1/2 CUP unsalted butter
- 1/4 TSP salt
- 1 CUP all purpose flour
- 3 eggs
- 1/4 sugar
- Pastry piping bag and star tip

Directions:
1. In a pot on your stovetop, bring the water to a boil, and drop in butter. Turn off heat and stir in salt, flour and eggs. Mix well until it balls up.
2. Using a pastry piping bag, transfer the dough into the pastry piping bag and attach the star tip. carefully squeeze mini sized portions, about 1.5 inches logo on the baking pan.
3. Transfer the baking pan onto the rack in the Turbo air fryer, and set it to 410F degrees and fry for 6 minutes.
4. Pour the 1/4 cup sugar into a small bowl, then roll the air fried churros in the sugar and serve.

Homemade Garlic Aioli
Servings: 8
Cooking Time: 0 Minutes

Ingredients:
- ½ cup mayonnaise
- 1 clove garlic minced
- 1 tablespoon lemon juice
- ¼ teaspoon kosher salt
- 2 teaspoons olive oil
- ¼ teaspoon pepper

Directions:
1. Mix all ingredients in a small bowl to combine.
2. Refrigerate at least 30 minutes before serving.
3. Notes
4. Makes approx 1 cup.
5. Keep in a tightly covered container in the fridge for about 2-3 days.

Air Fryer Frozen Mozzarella Sticks
Servings: 24
Cooking Time: 6 Minutes

Ingredients:
- 24 Frozen mozzarella sticks or bites this can be any brand of choice

Directions:
1. Preheat the air fryer at 180C/360F for 3 minutes.
2. Remove the frozen mozzarella sticks from its packaging and carefully arrange it in the

preheated air fryer basket in a single layer making sure to leave some spaces in between them
3. Cook at 180C/360F for 6 minutes or until crispy on the outside and cheese melted in the middle.
4. Serve immediately with marinara dipping sauce or pizza sauce. enjoy!
5. NOTES
6. PS: most recipe websites suggest cooking at 200C/400F, personally, I believe this would only cook the mozzarella sticks too quickly and explode during cooking.

Tips

I used Cosori 5.7l air fryer and was able to fit 24 frozen cheese pieces in the basket. If you are catering for more then be sure to cook them in batches.

Do not thaw before cooking and avoid stacking them so that they cook evenly Flip the cheese sticks halfway through the cooking time if need be, I did not need to do this

No need to spray the air fry basket with cooking oil for this recipe

Air Fryer Halloumi

Servings: 6
Cooking Time: 10-15 Minutes

Ingredients:
- 225g halloumi, cut into 6cm x 1cm thick slices
- 1 tsp olive oil
- 1 tsp smoked paprika, mixed herbs, or other flavourings (optional)

Directions:
1. Heat your air fryer on 200C for 2 mins. Carefully pat the halloumi dry using kitchen paper or a clean cloth, then brush or rub with oil. Season with salt and pepper and any flavourings, if using.
2. Put the halloumi in the air fryer basket and cook for 8 mins until beginning to brown. Flip over and cook for a further 2-5 mins until crisp and golden.

Air Fryer Acorn Squash

Servings: 4
Cooking Time: 30 Minutes

Ingredients:
- 2 medium acorn squash about 2 pounds
- 1 tablespoon olive oil
- ¼ teaspoon kosher salt or to taste
- 1 tablespoon butter
- 1 tablespoon brown sugar
- ⅛ teaspoon cinnamon

Directions:
1. Preheat the air fryer to 370°F.
2. Cut the squash in half and use a spoon to scrape out the seeds.
3. Brush the squash with olive oil and sprinkle with salt.
4. Place in the air fryer basket, cut side up, and cook 15 minutes.
5. Combine softened butter, brown sugar and cinnamon.
6. Open the air fryer and brush with the brown sugar mixture. Cook an additional 10-15 minutes or until the flesh is tender and slightly golden.

Notes

Preheat the air fryer so the initial blast of heat can caramelize the butter and seasonings right into the squash.

Leave enough space between portions so the air can circulate properly.

Keep leftover air fryer acorn squash in a covered container for up to 4 days.

Reheat in the air fryer or add to soups, stews, stir-fries, or even a morning smoothie!

Freeze cooled portions in a zippered bag for up to 4 weeks.

Air Fryer Hot Dogs

Servings: 4
Cooking Time: 5 Minutes

Ingredients:
- 4 Hot Dogs
- 4 Hot Dog Buns

Directions:
1. Take the hot dogs out of packaging, then cut a diagonal slits into each hot dog.
2. Place hot dogs in air fryer in a single layer. Air fry at 400 degrees F for 5-7 minutes cooking time.
3. Once hot dogs are done, use tongs or a fork to remove from the basket. Place hot dogs in bun, then place buns into air fryer basket.
4. Return hotdogs and buns to air fryer and air fry again at 400 degrees F for 1-2 minutes, until bun is a golden color.
5. Remove from air fryer basket and serve with favorite delicious toppings, such as ketchup, mustard, or BBQ sauce.

Air Fryer Biscuit Dough Pizzas

Servings: 8
Cooking Time: 10 Minutes

Ingredients:
- 1 can Grands! refrigerated biscuits (8 biscuits)
- 1 cup (240 ml) pizza sauce or tomato sauce
- 1 cup (113 g) shredded cheese
- salt , to taste
- black pepper , to taste
- OPTIONAL TOPPINGS
- Pepperoni, cooked Sausage, Bacon pieces, diced Ham, sliced or diced Tomatoes, Mushrooms, Pineapple, etc.
- OTHER SAUCE OPTIONS
- BBQ Sauce, Salsa, White (Alfredo) Sauce, Pesto, etc.
- EQUIPMENT
- Air Fryer
- Air Fryer Rack optional

Directions:

1. Separate the biscuits, then flatten and roll out each biscuit to 5-inches (13cm) wide.
2. Place in the air fryer basket/tray in a single layer (cook in batches if needed - do not top with sauce or toppings yet).
3. Air Fry at 330°F/166°C for 3 minutes. Flip the biscuit dough over. Continue to Air Fry at 330°F/166°C for another 3-4 minutes, or until cooked through.
4. Spread about 2 Tablespoons of sauce over each biscuit dough base. Then sprinkle about 2 Tablespoons of cheese on top. Add additional salt, pepper and other desired toppings.
5. Place the biscuit dough pizzas in the air fryer basket/tray in a single layer (cook in batches if needed). To keep your topping from flying around, place an air fryer rack over the pizzas.
6. Increase the heat and Air Fry the pizzas at 360°F/182°C for 2-5 minutes or until heated through and cheese is melted.

Air Fryer Italian Sausage

Servings: 2
Cooking Time: 11 Minutes

Ingredients:
- 2 sausages
- bun optional for serving

Directions:
1. Preheat the air fryer to 360°F.
2. Spread the sausage out in a single layer in the air fryer basket.
3. Cook for 5 minutes, then flip the sausage and cook an additional 5-6 minutes or until cooked through.

Notes
Preheat the air fryer for best results.
Do not poke the sausage before cooking, this will release all of the fats that keep sausages juicy.
Sausages can be sliced before air frying. More of the fats will drain this way.
Place parchment paper on the bottom of the air fryer tray when you add the sausage (never preheat with parchment paper) or basket for a quick and easy clean-up!

Air Fryer Mac & Cheese

Servings: 4-6
Cooking Time: 45 Minutes

Ingredients:
- 1/2 pound dry uncooked pasta (we used elbow macaroni)
- 2 cups whole milk
- 1 cup chicken stock
- 4 tablespoons butter
- 4 tablespoons cream cheese
- 8-ounce package sharp cheddar cheese, shredded
- 1 cup shredded mozzarella cheese
- 1/4 teaspoon kosher salt
- 1/4 teaspoon white pepper
- 1 teaspoon dry mustard
- Pinch Cayenne pepper
- Few grinds fresh nutmeg

Directions:
1. Preheat air fryer on 400 degrees F. for 10 minutes.
2. Rinse pasta under hot tap water for two minutes and drain.
3. Place milk, chicken stock, butter and cream cheese in a glass 4-cup or larger measuring cup and microwave until hot, and the butter melted, about 3-4 minutes. (This just needs to be hot enough to melt the butter and cream cheese, not boiling hot)
4. Mix drained pasta, hot liquid, cheddar, mozzarella, salt, pepper, mustard, cayenne and nutmeg in a large bowl then pour into the Air Fryer handled pan.
5. Spray a round parchment circle with pan spray and place sprayed side down over the macaroni mixture, pressing down to touch the mixture. Cover the top with foil and set into the heated air fryer and cook for 45 minutes.
6. Note: Air fryer wattages vary so check at 35 minutes and cook the additional 5-10 minutes as needed. Our air fryer is an 1800-watt air fryer and our macaroni and cheese took exactly 45 minutes.

Air Fryer Butternut Squash Soup

Servings: 4

Ingredients:
- Deselect All
- 1 1/2 pounds butternut squash (from about half of 1 large squash), peeled and cut into 1-inch pieces
- 2 medium carrots, cut into 1 1/2-inch pieces
- 1 orange bell pepper, stemmed, seeded and cut into 1-inch-thick slices
- 1/2 medium onion, cut into 4 wedges
- 3 tablespoons olive oil
- 3/4 teaspoon granulated garlic
- 1/2 teaspoon ground ginger
- 1/4 teaspoon dried thyme
- Kosher salt and freshly ground black pepper
- 3 cups low-sodium vegetable broth
- 1/2 cup heavy cream
- Roasted, salted pepitas, for serving
- Crème fraîche or full-fat plain yogurt, for serving
- Finely chopped chives, for serving

Directions:
1. Special equipment: a 6-quart air fryer
2. Preheat a 6-quart air fryer to 375 degrees F. Toss the butternut squash, carrots, bell pepper, onion, olive oil, granulated garlic, ginger, thyme, 1 1/2 teaspoons salt and several grinds of black pepper together in a large bowl until well combined. Transfer to the air fryer basket. Fry until golden brown and tender, tossing halfway through, about 20 minutes.
3. Transfer the browned vegetables to a large pot or Dutch oven and add the broth and cream. Use an immersion blender to blend the mixture on medium-high until very smooth. (Alternatively, blend the mixture in a standard blender, first letting it cool for 5 minutes, then transferring it to the blender, filling only halfway. Put the lid on, leaving one corner open. Cover the lid with a kitchen towel to catch splatters, and pulse until very smooth, scrapping down the sides of the blender carafe with a rubber

spatula as needed; pour the blended mixture back into the pot.)
4. Cook the soup over medium-low heat, stirring occasionally, until the mixture is just simmering, about 5 minutes. Taste and adjust the seasoning with salt and pepper. Ladle into bowls and top with pepitas, drizzle with crème fraîche or yogurt and sprinkle with chives.

Air Fryer Sausage Recipe
Servings: 5
Cooking Time: 7 Minutes
Ingredients:
- 5 3.8-oz Italian sausage links

Directions:
1. Preheat the air fryer to 400 degrees F (204 degrees C). (For air fryers, it's also fine if you skip preheating.)
2. Arrange Italian sausage in the air fryer basket in a single layer, with space between the links.
3. Cook for 7-8 minutes, until golden brown and Internal temperature reaches 160 degrees F (71 degrees C).

Smoked Sausage In The Air Fryer
Servings: 4
Cooking Time: 6 Minutes
Ingredients:
- One package of smoked sausage
- Bbq sauce for serving (optional)

Directions:
1. Preheat your air fryer to 370 degrees F.
2. Meanwhile, cut the sausage into 1-1.5" pieces.
3. Air fry the sausage for 5-6 minutes, shaking the basket once halfway.
4. Serve immediately with bbq sauce for dipping if desired.

Air Fryer Fried Rice
Servings: 4
Cooking Time: 20 Minutes
Ingredients:
- 300g chicken tenderloins
- 4 rashers rindless bacon
- 450g packet microwave long-grain rice
- 2 tbsp oyster sauce
- 2 tbsp light soy sauce
- 1 tsp sesame oil
- 3 tsp finely grated fresh ginger
- 2 eggs, lightly whisked
- 120g (3/4 cup) frozen peas
- 2 green shallots, sliced
- 1 long fresh red chilli, thinly sliced
- Oyster sauce, to drizzle
- Select all ingredients

Directions:
1. Preheat the air fryer to 180C. Place the chicken and bacon on the air fryer rack. Cook for 8 minutes or until cooked through. Transfer to a plate and set aside to cool slightly. Slice the chicken and chop the bacon.
2. Meanwhile, use your fingers to separate the rice grains in the packet. Microwave the rice for 1 minute. Transfer to a round 20cm, high-sided ovenproof dish or cake pan. Add the oyster sauce, soy sauce, sesame oil, ginger and 2 tablespoons water. Stir to combine.
3. Place the dish or pan in the air fryer. Cook for 5 minutes or until the rice is tender. Stir through the egg, peas, chicken and half of the bacon. Cook for 3 minutes or until the egg is cooked through. Stir in half the shallot and season with salt and white pepper.
4. Serve sprinkled with chilli, remaining shallot, remaining bacon and extra oyster sauce.

3 Ingredient Dog Treats

Servings: 50
Cooking Time: 4 Hr

Ingredients:
- 2 cups rolled oats
- ½ cup peanut butter (only ingredient should be peanuts)
- ½ cup fruit or vegetable purée (apple, banana, sweet potato, or pumpkin are all great options)
- Items Needed
- Food processor
- Parchment paper
- Cookie cutters (optional)

Directions:
1. Place the oats in a food processor and blend until the oats turn into oat flour.
2. Add the peanut butter and fruit or vegetable purée of choice and blend until a dough forms.
3. Roll dough out to ¼-inch thickness between parchment paper so it doesn't stick.
4. Cut the dough out into 2-inch sized shapes using cookie cutters or a knife.
5. Place the treats evenly between the Food Dehydrator trays.
6. Set temperature to 145°F and time to 4 hours, then press Start/Stop.
7. Remove when done, cool to room temperature on the trays, then serve to your pet.

Air Fryer Frozen Dumplings

Servings: 4
Cooking Time: 14 Minutes

Ingredients:
- 12 Frozen Dumplings
- oil spray, to coat the dumplings
- optional dipping sauce(soy sauce & sesame seed oil, hoisin, sweet & sour, hot mustard, hot sauce, etc.)
- EQUIPMENT
- Air Fryer
- Oil Sprayer

Directions:
1. Place the frozen dumplings in the air fryer basket and spread out into a single even layer. Spray liberally with oil to completely coat the dumplings. If you don't use oil spray the dumplings will cook dry and hard.
2. Air Fry at 380°F/193°C for about 6-8 minutes. Check after the first 6 minutes to make sure they don't burn. Some air fryers cook hotter than others.
3. Flip the dumplings over and continue to Air Fry at 380°F/193°C for another 2-6 minutes if needed until crispy on the outside OR until they are cooked to your preferred doneness.
4. Allow them to cool for a bit. Serve with soy sauce or your favorite dip.

NOTES

Air Frying Tips and Notes:

Cook Frozen - Do not thaw first.

Turn as needed. Don't overcrowd the air fryer basket.

Recipe timing is based on a non-preheated air fryer. If cooking in multiple batches back to back, the following batches may cook a little quicker.

Recipes were tested in 3.7 to 6 qt. air fryers. If using a larger air fryer, they might cook quicker so adjust cooking time.

Remember to set a timer to flip/turn as directed in recipe.

SNACKS & APPETIZERS RECIPES

Homemade Air Fryer Tater Tots

Servings: 8
Cooking Time: 20 Minutes

Ingredients:
- 1 16 ounce bag of frozen shredded hash browns
- 2 tablespoons olive oil
- 2 tablespoons flour
- 3 cloves garlic minced
- 1 teaspoon dried Italian seasoning
- ½ teaspoon kosher salt
- ¼ cup grated parmesan cheese

Directions:
1. Pulse hashbrowns in a food processor until finely chopped (don't allow them to become mashed potatoes).
2. Gently mix the potatoes with olive oil, flour, garlic, & seasoning.
3. Scoop tablespoon-sized amounts of the mixture and form into 1" tater tots. Place in the air fryer in a single layer, evenly spaced.
4. Spray them with olive oil or cooking spray. Air fry tater tots at 375°F for 15-18 minutes until crispy and golden brown, shaking the air fryer basket once during cooking.
5. Remove tots from the fryer, and sprinkle with shredded parmesan and seasoning. Serve warm.

Notes
For extra garlicky tater tots add a teaspoon of garlic powder.
For cheesy tots, add ¼-½ cup parmesan cheese to the tater tot mixture.
Store in an airtight container in the fridge for up to 5 days.

Air Fryer Frozen French Fries

Servings: 4
Cooking Time: 15 Minutes

Ingredients:
- 1 pound (454 g) frozen french fries
- Kosher salt or sea salt, to taste
- ground black pepper, to taste optional
- EQUIPMENT
- Air Fryer

Directions:
1. Place the frozen fries in air fryer basket and spread them evenly over the basket. You don't need to spray extra oil.
2. Air fry the frozen fries at 400°F/205°C for about 15 minutes (about 10 minutes for thin cut fries). About halfway through cooking, shake the basket and gently turn the fries. Try not to break them. For crisper, evenly cooked fries, turn them multiples times while cooking.
3. Air Fry for additional 1-3 minutes to crisp to your preferred liking. Season with salt and pepper if desired.

NOTES
No Oil Necessary. Cook Fries Frozen - Do not thaw first.
Shake several times for even cooking & Don't overcrowd fryer basket.
If cooking in multiple batches, the first batch will take longer to cook if Air Fryer is not already pre-heated.
Recipes were cooked in 3-4 qt air fryers. If using a larger air fryer, the recipe might require more time.
Remember to set a timer to shake/flip/toss the food as directed in recipe.

Air-fryer Pickle Chips

Servings: 6

Ingredients:
- 2 cup sliced dill pickles
- 3 tablespoon cornstarch
- ½ teaspoon salt
- ¼ teaspoon black pepper
- ½ cup buttermilk
- 2 tablespoon Sriracha sauce
- 1 ¼ cup panko bread crumbs
- 1 tablespoon vegetable oil
- ½ cup ranch salad dressing

Directions:
1. Preheat air-fryer to 400°F. Lay pickle slices on a paper-towel lined baking sheet; pat dry.
2. In a shallow dish combine cornstarch, salt, and pepper. In another shallow dish combine buttermilk and 1 Tbsp. Sriracha. In a third shallow dish combine panko and oil.
3. Working in batches, gently coat dried pickle slices in cornstarch mixture, shaking off excess, then coat in buttermilk mixture. Roll in panko to coat.
4. Place breaded pickle slices in basket (do not overcrowd). Cook for 6 to 8 minutes or until golden brown. Keep cooked slices in a 200°F oven while cooking the remaining slices.
5. Meanwhile, in a small bowl combine ranch dressing and remaining 1 Tbsp. Sriracha.
6. Serve pickle chips immediately with spicy ranch.

Air Fryer Avocado Fries
Servings: 4
Cooking Time: 8 Minutes

Ingredients:
- 2 large avocados sliced
- 1 cup panko breadcrumbs
- 1/2 cup Italian breadcrumbs
- 1/4 cup all purpose flour
- 1 egg beaten
- 1/2 teaspoon ground black pepper
- 1/2 teaspoon garlic powder
- 1/4 teaspoon sea salt
- 1 teaspoon avocado spray

Directions:
1. Preheat the air fryer to 370 degrees Fahrenheit.
2. Add the Italian breadcrumbs, flour, black pepper, garlic powder, and sea salt into a rimmed dish.
3. Add the panko breadcrumbs to a rimmed dish.
4. Add the beaten egg to a small bowl.
5. Create a dipping station by setting each dish next to each other in an assembly line type setup.
6. Begin by rolling an avocado slice in the flour, tapping to remove any excess flour from the slice. Take the flour dipped avocado slice and place it into the egg mixture, then dip into the breadcrumbs mixture, and finally the panko breadcrumbs last.
7. Repeat the process with all of the remaining avocado slices.
8. Prepare the air fryer basket with avocado oil spray.
9. Carefully line the breaded avocados in a single layer in the air fryer basket. Make sure to leave room in between each slice to allow for complete air circulation.
10. Spray the avocado slices with a light coat of avocado oil, and then air fry at 370 degrees Fahrenheit for 7-8 minutes, flipping them halfway through.
11. Serve with your favorite dipping sauce.

NOTES

All air fryers cook a little differently. This recipe was made using a 5.8 qt basket style Cosori air fryer. If you are using a different brand of air fryer, make sure you do a "test run" of this recipe to see if you need to adjust the cooking time.

Dipping sauces are a great way to add different flavors to this recipe. I think that ranch dressing, BBQ sauce, or even your favorite hot sauce or spicy sauce are the perfect flavor enhancers.

Add a little bit of parmesan cheese into the panko mixture for simple salty addition.

Squeeze a little bit of lime juice over the top of the avocados after they're cooked in the air fryer. This gives a tasty citrus flavor! (Lemon juice works well, too!)

Air Fryer Home Fries
Servings: 4
Cooking Time: 20 Minutes

Ingredients:
- 1 1/2 pounds russet potatoes
- 2 Tablespoons olive oil
- 1/4 cup onion chopped
- 1/3 cup bell pepper red, chopped
- 1 teaspoon garlic salt
- 1 teaspoon paprika
- 1/2 teaspoon ground black pepper

Directions:
1. Peel and rinse potatoes in cold water to remove excess starch.
2. Then cut them into 1-inch cubes.
3. Lay them out on a cutting board covered with a paper towel or a clean towel to absorb excess moisture.
4. Combine in a medium bowl the olive oil, red bell pepper and chopped onion.
5. Next add the garlic salt, paprika and black pepper into the mixing bowl.
6. Toss all the ingredients together until fully coated.
7. Place the seasoned home fries into the air fryer basket in a single layer allowing adequate space so they cook evenly.
8. Cook at 400 degrees F for 20 minutes. Shaking the basket halfway through the air frying cooking process.
9. Potatoes will be crispy and golden brown when done.
10. Serve immediately while hot.

NOTES
I make this recipe in my Cosori 5.8-quart air fryer. Depending on your type of air fryer, size and wattages, cook time may need to be adjusted an additional minute or two.
Because these fries go with almost any sauce, it's really a taste preference. I love spicy chipotle sauce, ranch dressing, tangy western sauce, blue cheese dressing, creamy cheese sauce, or with the original sauce ketchup.
I love topping these fries with a bit of parmesan cheese, salsa, chili, shredded cheeses, sour cream or hot sauce.

Air Fryer Green Beans
Servings: 4
Cooking Time: 6 Minutes

Ingredients:
- 1 lb green beans trimmed
- 2 tablespoons olive oil
- 1/2 teaspoon salt
- 1/2 teaspoon pepper

Directions:
1. Preheat the air fryer to 190C/375F.
2. In a mixing bowl, add the trimmed beans then toss through the olive oil, salt, and pepper.
3. Add a single layer of the beans to the air fryer basket and air fry for 8 minutes, shaking halfway through. Repeat the process until all the beans are cooked.
4. Sprinkle with parmesan cheese and add a squeeze of lemon juice.

Notes
TO STORE: Leftovers can be stored in the refrigerator, covered, for up to 5 days.
TO FREEZE: Place the cooked and cooled beans in a ziplock bag and store them in the freezer for up to 6 months.
TO REHEAT: Either microwave for a few seconds or reheat in the air fryer for 1-2 minutes.

Air Fryer Sweet Potato Fries
Servings: 2
Cooking Time: 12 Minutes

Ingredients:
- 2 medium sweet potatoes peeled
- 2 teaspoons olive oil
- ½ teaspoon salt
- ¼ teaspoon garlic powder
- ¼ teaspoon paprika
- ⅛ teaspoon black pepper

Directions:
1. Preheat the air fryer to 380°F. Peel the sweet potatoes, then slice each potato into even 1/4 inch thick sticks.

2. Place the sweet potatoes in a large mixing bowl, and toss with olive oil, salt, garlic powder, paprika and black pepper.
3. Cook in 2 or 3 batches, depending on the size of your basket without overcrowding the pan until they're crispy. I recommend 12 minutes, turning half way. This may vary based on your air fryer.
4. Serve immediately with your favorite dipping sauce.

Notes

Storage: Store any leftovers in an airtight container. They will last about 3-4 days in the fridge. To reheat, just place in the air fryer at 360°F for 1-2 minutes or in a toaster oven. You can also reheat in the microwave but the potatoes will be soft if heated in the microwave.
Substitutes: For best results, follow the recipe as is. However you can switch out the spices and use a different oil
Equipment: I used the NuWave Air Fryer to make this recipe. It's easy to use with guides on the appliance, easy to clean up and I've been very happy with the results!

Air Fryer French Fries

Servings: 4
Cooking Time: 20 Minutes

Ingredients:
- 2 medium sized russet potatoes
- 1 tablespoon olive oil
- 1 teaspoon Italian seasoning
- 2 tablespoons Parmesan cheese, grated
- 1/2 teaspoon salt
- 1/4 teaspoon pepper

Directions:
1. Preheat the air fryer to 380 degrees Fahrenheit. Slice the potatoes using a fry cutter, or slice them into 1/4-inch strips.
2. Rinse the potato slices in cold water and pat dry with a paper towel.
3. In a medium-sized bowl toss with olive oil, Italian seasoning, Parmesan cheese, salt, and pepper.
4. Place the fries into the basket of the air fryer in a single layer. Cook for 15-20 minutes or until golden brown.
5. Toss the fries halfway through the cooking process to ensure the fries get evenly cooked.
6. Serve with ketchup or fry sauce.

Homemade Oven Chips

Servings: 2
Cooking Time: 30 Minutes

Ingredients:
- 250 g King Edward potatoes
- low calorie cooking spray

Directions:
1. ACTIFRY **Directions:**
2. Peel the potatoes, cut into 1cm slices, and then into 1cm strips to make chips. You can cut them thinner or fatter, but this will change the amount of cooking they need so adjust the time accordingly.
3. Place the potatoes into a large bowl of cold water and rinse well.
4. Drain the water, pat dry with some kitchen towel and spray with low calorie cooking spray until they are all covered.
5. Place into the Tefal Actifry, spray again with low calorie cooking spray, close the lid and set to cook for 15 minutes.
6. After 15 minutes, open the lid, toss, and spray with more low calorie cooking spray. Set to cook for a further 15 minutes. Serve immediately with salt and vinegar if desired!
7. OVEN **Directions:**
8. Preheat the oven to 200°C. Peel the potatoes, cut into 1cm slices, and then into 1cm strips to make chips. You can cut them thinner or fatter, but this will change the amount of cooking they need so adjust the time accordingly.
9. Place the potatoes into a large bowl of cold water and rinse well.

10. Drain the water, pat dry with some kitchen towel and spray with low calorie cooking spray until they are all covered.
11. Place onto a non-stick baking tray and spray with low calorie cooking spray. Place into the oven for 20 minutes.
12. After 20 minutes, turn the chips over on the baking tray, spray with low calorie cooking spray again and cook for a further 15-20 minutes until golden. Serve immediately with salt and vinegar if desired!

Air Fryer Pasta Chips
Servings: 4
Cooking Time: 20 Minutes

Ingredients:
- 8 oz. (227 g) dried Bowtie (Farfalle) Pasta, or pasta shape of choice
- 1 Tablespoon (15 ml) Olive Oil or Vegetable Oil
- 1 teaspoon (5 ml) Garlic Powder
- 1/3 cup (35 g) Parmesan Cheese
- 1/2 teaspoon (2.5 ml) Kosher Salt , or to taste
- Optional - additional seasonings of choice - Italian seasoning , dried basil, onion powder, etc.
- EQUIPMENT
- Air Fryer

Directions:
1. In a large pot of salted boiling water, cook the pasta to package directions. Cook until it is tender (it crisps up best if it is cooked a little beyond al dente).
2. Drain the pasta and put in a bowl. Toss with the olive oil, garlic powder, parmesan cheese, and salt (it should be well seasoned).
3. Cooking in batches if needed, put just a single layer of the seasoned pasta in the air fryer basket/tray. (For most air fryers, cook in batches to avoid overcrowding the basket/tray. For best results air fry in just a single layer.)
4. Air Fry at 380°F/195°C for 7-10 minutes, shaking and stirring the pasta every 2-3 minutes making sure to separate any pasta sticking together. (Shaking often helps them crispy evenly and not burnt.) Cook until the pasta is golden and crispy to your liking. Timing will vary depending on your air fryer model, type of pasta you're cooking and preferred texture.
5. If cooking in batches, the next batches might cook quicker because the air fryer is already hot. Serve with warmed marinara sauce or sauce of choice.

Air Fryer Frozen Onion Rings
Servings: 4
Cooking Time: 20 Minutes

Ingredients:
- 1- 14 ounce bag frozen onion rings
- non-stick cooking spray

Directions:
1. Layer half of the bag of frozen onion rings into the basket of the air fryer. Make sure to layer them in one layer making sure not to overlap the onion rings.
2. Lightly spray the onion rings with non-stick cooking spray. This gives them extra crispiness.
3. Close the air fryer and cook at 400 degrees Fahrenheit for 8-10 minutes.
4. Halfway through the cooking process, open the basket and flip the onion rings. Continue to cook to desired crispness.
5. Remove the cooked onion rings from the basket and repeat these steps for the remaining frozen onion rings.
6. Enjoy right away with your favorite dipping sauce!

Air Fryer Chips

Servings: 2
Cooking Time: 10-30 Minutes

Ingredients:
- 2 large potatoes (approximately 450g/1lb), preferably a waxy variety
- 1 tbsp olive oil
- salt, to taste

Directions:
1. Leaving the skins on, cut the potatoes into roughly 1cm/½in thick chips. Toss with the olive oil and a generous amount of salt.
2. Air-fry for 20–30 minutes at 180C, tossing every 10 minutes or so until the chips are crisp and golden, making sure they don't stick to the bottom of the basket towards the beginning of cooking.
3. Recipe Tips
4. If you have time, soak the chips for up to 30 minutes to extract some of the starch before frying. You can also par-boil the chips for 8–10 minutes to cut the cooking time and make really fluffy chips. This recipe was tested in a 3.2 litre/5½ pint basket air fryer, but it will also work in a model fitted with a stirring paddle – in this case, you won't need to toss the chips during cooking.

Air Fryer Zucchini Chips

Servings: 4
Cooking Time: 8 Minutes

Ingredients:
- 1 medium-sized zucchini
- 1/2 cup panko breadcrumbs
- 1/2 teaspoon garlic powder
- 1/4 teaspoon onion powder
- 1 egg
- 3 tablespoons flour

Directions:
1. Cut zucchini into thin slices, approximately 1/4 inches.
2. Mix panko breadcrumbs, garlic powder, and onion powder in a bowl.
3. Whisk one egg into a separate bowl and put the flour in a third bowl.
4. Dip zucchini into the flour, then the egg, then the breadcrumbs.
5. Place the breaded zucchini in an air fryer in a single layer and cook at 380 degrees for 7-9 minutes, flipping halfway.
6. Enjoy immediately.

Air Fryer Crunchy Chili-spiced Chickpeas

Servings: 2-4

Ingredients:
- 1 (15-oz.) can chickpeas, rinsed and drained
- 1 tbsp. extra-virgin olive oil
- 2 tsp. chili powder
- 1/4 tsp. kosher salt
- Finely grated lime zest, for serving

Directions:
1. Dry chickpeas very well with paper towels. In a medium bowl, toss chickpeas, oil, chili powder, and salt.
2. Transfer chickpea mixture to an air-fryer basket, scraping bowl to get all of the oil. Cook at 370° until crispy and golden brown, 10 to 14 minutes.
3. Serve chickpeas warm or at room temperature. Grate lime zest over top.

Air Fryer Truffle Fries

Servings: 4
Cooking Time: 20 Minutes

Ingredients:
- 4 medium Russett potatoes
- 3 Tablespoons parsley chopped, fresh
- 3 Tablespoons truffle oil white
- 1/2 teaspoon sea salt truffle or Kosher
- 1/2 cup parmesan cheese freshly shredded

Directions:
1. Carefully remove skin on potatoes and slice them lengthwise into fries.
2. Place the potatoes into a bowl of ice water and allow them to soak for 10 minutes (this will make crispy potatoes).
3. While the fries are soaking, finely chop the parsley and set aside.

4. Drain the potatoes and use paper towels or a clean kitchen towel to remove any excess water from the potatoes.
5. Transfer the potatoes to a medium-sized mixing bowl.
6. Toss the fries with truffle oil and salt. Mix until the fries are fully coated.
7. Place the truffle fries into the air fryer basket and air fry at 350 degrees F for 20 minutes, flipping the fries halfway through the cooking process.
8. Once fried, put the fries into a medium sized mixing bowl and coat with the parsley and parmesan. Mix well.
9. Serve immediately while hot.

NOTES

Optional Favorite Dipping Sauce: Ketchup, ranch dressing, blue cheese dressing, honey mustard sauce or creamed horseradish.

Optional Favorite Toppings: Chopped chives, melty cheese sauce, fresh thyme or avocado slices.

Cooking Tips: If you make fries in batches place them on a wire rack so they remain crispy.

Substitutions: Use black truffle oil, olive oil or avocado oil if you do not have white truffle oil.

Air Fryer Potato Chips

Servings: 2
Cooking Time: 20 Minutes

Ingredients:
- 1 medium potato (russet, yellow, or gold)
- about 1 Tablespoon (30ml) oil spray
- salt , to taste
- pepper , to taste
- optional: ground cumin , garlic powder or onion powder or paprika
- Mandoline optional
- Cut-Resistant gloves optional

Directions:
1. Pre-heat Air Fryer at 340°F/170°C for 5 minutes.
2. Slice potato into 1/8" thin slices. (A mandoline with cut-resistant gloves makes this step quick & even). Discard the small end pieces.
3. Optional - Add potato slices to bowl of cold water for at least 20 minutes. Remove potato slices and pat dry with towel.
4. Place potato slices in a bowl and spray with oil, season with salt, pepper or optional spices. Toss potatoes to evenly coat all sides with the oil and seasonings.
5. Spray the air fryer basket/tray with oil to minimize sticking. Lay potato slices in single layer, trying to not overlap slices.
6. Initial Browning: Air Fry at 340°F/170°C for 10 minutes. Flip and separate any touching slices.
7. Continue to Air Fry at 340°F/170°C for 3-5 minutes increments or until they start to crisp on the edges. Separate the potatoes so they don't stick together and this helps the chips crisp on both sides. Look for crispy brown sides because this is what makes them crunchy. But don't let them burn. Check out our photos for reference.
8. Finishing: When you see crisp brown edges, reduce heat to 280°F/140°C and Air Fry for another 2-5 minutes or until they are dry. The chips will become crunchier when they cool.
9. If some of the chips are a still little chewy, then remove the crunchy ones and continue to Air Fry the chewy chips at 280°F/140°C for another 3 minutes or until crispy.

NOTES

Cooking times will vary depending on the thickness of your potatoes, how much you cook and the size of your air fryer. Try to choose a wider potato, as the slices will shrink quite a bit. The smaller the slices are, the harder they are to handle and flip.

Avoid cooking too many slices in multiple layers because you will get un-even cooking. It's better to air fry single layers in multiple batches than one big batch.

Air Fryer Roasted Butternut Squash & Kale Salad With Balsamic-maple Dressing

Servings: 4-6

Ingredients:
- 1 medium butternut squash (about 2 lb.), peeled, seeded, and cut into 1" pieces (about 6 c.)
- 2 tbsp. plus 2 tsp. extra-virgin olive oil
- 1 tsp. kosher salt, divided, plus more
- 1/4 tsp. freshly ground black pepper
- 2 tbsp. balsamic vinegar
- 2 tsp. maple syrup
- 1 tsp. Dijon mustard
- 1 bunch of curly kale, stems removed, leaves roughly chopped (about 6 packed c.)
- 1/4 c. dried cranberries
- 2 tbsp. raw pumpkin seeds (pepitas)
- 2 oz. goat cheese

Directions:
1. In a large bowl, toss squash, 2 teaspoons oil, 1/2 teaspoon salt, and 1/4 teaspoon pepper. Scrape into an air-fryer basket; reserve bowl. Cook at 400°, shaking basket or tossing squash a few times, until squash is tender and golden, about 15 minutes.
2. Meanwhile, in reserved bowl, whisk vinegar, syrup, mustard, 1/2 teaspoon salt, and remaining 2 tbsp. oil. Add kale and massage into dressing to soften a bit.
3. Transfer squash to bowl with kale. Add cranberries and pepitas and toss to combine; season with salt and pepper. Crumble goat cheese over and gently toss into salad.

Air Fryer Flower Fries

Servings: 12

Ingredients:
- Deselect All
- 12 small yellow potatoes, such as baby gold (about 1 pound)
- Olive oil spray
- 1 teaspoon kosher salt
- 6 teaspoons ranch dressing, plus more for serving
- 6 red and yellow cherry tomatoes, halved
- Baby arugula, for serving

Directions:
1. Special equipment: a 16-slice thin apple slicer, a melon baller, a 6-quart air fryer
2. Line up the potatoes and slice one end from each, taking off more or less to ensure that all the potatoes are the same length. (Reserve all the potato scraps: you can toss them with salt and oil to air fry later.)
3. Stand up each potato on its flat side. Working with 1 potato at a time, place a 16-slice thin apple slicer over the center of the rounded end. Carefully push the slicer down using a see-sawing motion until the blades are 1/4 inch from the bottom of the potato. Don't push firmly straight down or you could accidentally slice through the entire potato. Remove the slicer by grasping the sides with both hands and firmly pushing your thumbs into the center of the potato. Use a melon baller to scoop out three-fourths of that center.
4. Thoroughly coat the potatoes all over with olive oil spray and season with the salt. Add them flat-sides down to a 6-quart air fryer. Cook at 380 degrees F until the petals are crispy and golden brown, 14 to 17 minutes depending on the size of your potatoes (see Cook's Note). Remove the air fryer basket, wait until the potatoes are cool enough to handle (about 1 minute) and gently pluck them out of the basket with your hands. Fill each center with 1/2 teaspoon ranch dressing and nestle half a cherry tomato on top, dome-side up. Arrange the potato flowers on a bed of baby arugula and serve with more ranch for dipping.
5. Cook's Note
6. Settings may vary on your air fryer depending on the model. Please refer to the manufacturer's guide.

Crispy Air Fryer French Fries

Servings: 3-4
Cooking Time: 12 Minutes

Ingredients:
- 2 medium russet potatoes, scrubbed
- 1 tablespoon olive oil
- 1/4 teaspoon salt
- 1/4 teaspoon garlic powder (optional)
- pinch of black pepper, to taste
- flaked sea salt, for serving

Directions:
1. Preheat the air fryer on 375 F for 5 minutes.
2. Slice the potatoes into long strips (french fry shape), roughly 1/4-inch thick. (I keep the skin on but you can peel the skin if you prefer).
3. Transfer sliced potatoes into a large bowl and add olive oil, salt, garlic powder (optional), and pepper. Toss to coat.
4. Place a single layer of potatoes into the air fryer basket and cook for 12-13 minutes, until crispy and golden. Do not overlap the potatoes as they will not cook evenly and crispy. I usually have to do this in 2 batches for the size of my air fryer.
5. Serve immediately with some flaked sea salt on top and a side of ketchup, spicy mayo or other dipping sauce.

NOTES
Equipment used: I used the Philips Digital Turbostar Air Fryer. We love it and have only good things to say about it.
How to double the recipe: You can double or triple the recipe, but you will have to make it in batches. To get tender but crispy french fries, you need to place them in the air fryer basket in one layer. If you start stacking them up and overcrowding the basket, they will not cook evenly and you may not get that crispy texture.
How to bake in the oven: To bake in the oven instead, spread the fries in an even layer on a large baking sheet. Bake for 25-30 minutes at 425 F, flipping the fries over halfway.

Air Fryer Fried Pickles

Servings: 6

Ingredients:
- Deselect All
- Pickles:
- One 16-ounce jar dill pickle chips
- 1/2 cup all-purpose flour
- 1/4 teaspoon ground cayenne pepper
- 1 1/2 teaspoons Cajun seasoning
- 1 cup buttermilk
- A couple of dashes hot sauce
- 1 1/2 cups panko
- 1 teaspoon Italian seasoning
- Kosher salt
- 1 tablespoon olive oil
- Dipping sauce:
- 1/2 cup mayonnaise
- 4 teaspoons ketchup
- 1 teaspoon prepared horseradish
- 1/2 teaspoon Cajun seasoning

Directions:
1. For the pickles: Preheat a 3.5-quart air fryer to 390 degrees F. Set a wire rack inside a baking sheet.
2. Drain the pickles and spread them out on a paper towel-lined baking sheet. Pat dry with more paper towels, pressing gently to remove as much moisture as possible. Eliminate any pickles with large holes or ones that are very thin.
3. Set up a breading station using 3 medium bowls: Whisk together the flour, cayenne and 1/2 teaspoon Cajun seasoning in one bowl. In the second bowl combine the buttermilk and hot sauce. In the last combine the panko, Italian seasoning, the remaining 1 teaspoon Cajun seasoning and 1/2 teaspoon salt. Drizzle in the oil and use your hands to toss and coat the panko.
4. Working in small batches, bread the pickles: First, toss a handful of pickles in the flour mixture, shaking off any excess. Then dunk them in the buttermilk mixture to completely coat, shaking to remove any excess. Finally, toss them in the panko,

pressing gently to make it adhere. Arrange the breaded pickles on the prepared baking sheet and repeat until all the pickles are breaded.
5. Arrange one-third of the breaded pickles in the basket of the air fryer in a single layer. Cook for 8 minutes, the pickles will be very crunchy and browned on both sides. Remove to a serving plate and repeat with the remaining two batches of pickles.
6. For the dipping sauce: Meanwhile, whisk together the mayonnaise, ketchup, horseradish and Cajun seasoning in small bowl.
7. Serve the warm pickles with the dipping sauce or use them and the dipping sauce to top your favorite burger.

Air Fryer Carrot Fries
Servings: 2-3
Cooking Time: 14 Minutes

Ingredients:
- 4-5 carrots, peeled
- 2 teaspoon cornstarch
- ½ teaspoon parsley
- ½ teaspoon garlic powder
- ¼ teaspoon salt
- 1 tablespoon olive oil
- ½ tablespoon grated parmesan

Directions:
1. Preheat your air fryer to 400 degrees F.
2. Peel your carrots. Cut each carrot in half to make shorter fries. Then cut them lengthwise in half and then half them again lengthwise. They should all be about the same size for even cooking.
3. In a small bowl combine the cornstarch, parsley, garlic powder, and salt. Place your carrots in a dish and drizzle your olive oil over them. Next, sprinkle the seasoning over the carrots, mixing them till they are coated evenly.
4. Place them in a single layer in your air fryer basket. Cook for 13 to 15 minutes. They should be fork tender but hold their shape when held up. Let them rest for just a few minutes, allowing them to crisp up a little bit more. Place them on a plate and sprinkle with parmesan cheese. Serve immediately.

NOTES
HOW TO REHEAT CARROT FRIES IN THE AIR FRYER
Preheat the air fryer to 350 degrees F.
Lay the leftover carrot fries in a single layer in the air fryer basket.
Cook for 3 to 4 minutes until heated through.

Air Fryer Roasted Chickpeas
Servings: 2
Cooking Time: 15 Minutes

Ingredients:
- 1 (15 oz) can chickpeas drained and rinsed
- 1/4-1/2 tsp sea salt
- 2 tsp olive oil
- Spices:
- 1/2 tsp smoked paprika or regular paprika
- 1/4-1/2 tsp ground cumin
- 1/4 tsp onion powder
- 1/4 tsp garlic powder
- 1/4 tsp curry powder
- 1/8 tsp cayenne pepper (optional)

Directions:
1. You can watch the video in the post for visual instructions.
2. In a small/medium bowl combine all spices and stir with a spoon. Set aside.
3. Drain and rinse chickpeas, then pat dry with a clean kitchen towel or paper towel. Some skins will fall off, and you can simply discard them. Add the chickpeas to a bowl and toss with the olive oil and salt.
4. Air fryer Directions:
5. Transfer the chickpeas to the air fryer basket. Set the timer to 15 minutes and 380 °F (195 °C). I didn't preheat my air fryer.
6. Cook for 5 minutes, shake the basket once, cook for a further 5 minutes and shake again. Mine were crunchy after 14 minutes, but you can leave them in for a further minute.
7. Remove the chickpeas from the air fryer and add them to the bowl you used to toss them

with oil. Spray with a little additional cooking spray (to help the spices adhere to the chickpeas). Then, add the spices and toss well to combine.

8. Oven Directions:
9. Preheat the oven to 375 °F (190 °C) and line a baking sheet with parchment paper. Transfer the chickpeas to the baking sheet. Roast them for 35 to 45 minutes, stirring halfway through.
10. Remove the chickpeas from the oven and add them to the bowl you used to toss them with oil. Spray with a little additional cooking spray, then, add the spices and toss well to combine.
11. Enjoy! Store in a glass container (jar) at room temperature for a couple of days. They taste best freshly made.

Notes
You can add a little brown sugar or coconut sugar to the spice mix for more flavor (optional). The chickpeas are even more crunchy if you remove the skins.

Air Fryer Kale Chips

Servings: 4
Cooking Time: 5 Minutes

Ingredients:
- BASIC AIR FRYER KALE CHIPS:
- 1 lb Curly Kale
- 1 tbsp Olive oil
- 1/2 tsp Sea salt
- LEMON GARLIC:
- 2 tbsp Lemon juice
- 2 tsp Lemon zest
- 1 tsp Garlic powder
- CHILI LIME:
- 4 tsp Lime juice
- 2 tsp Chili powder
- 1/2 tsp Garlic powder
- TACO:
- 4 tsp Taco Seasoning
- RANCH:
- 4 tsp Ranch seasoning
- BBQ:
- 3 tbsp BBQ sauce
- CAJUN:
- 1 tbsp Cajun seasoning
- SALT AND VINEGAR:
- 3 tbsp White vinegar
- NACHO CHEESE:
- 3 tbsp Cheddar cheese powder
- 1/4 tsp Cumin
- 1/4 tsp Garlic powder
- 1/4 tsp Onion powder
- 1/2 tsp Chili powder
- 1/4 tsp Paprika
- FLAMIN' HOT:
- 2 tbsp Cheddar cheese powder
- 2-3 tbsp Hot sauce
- 1/2 tsp Garlic powder
- SOUR CREAM AND ONION:
- 2 tbsp Buttermilk powder
- 1/2 tbsp Onion powder
- 2 tsp Dried parsley

Directions:
1. Wash kale and dry thoroughly. (Kale chips will take longer to crisp up if you don't dry the kale well).
2. Use a sharp knife to slice around the tough stem of each kale leaf. Discard stem. Roughly chop kale into bite-sized pieces.
3. Place kale in a large mixing bowl. Add the olive oil and salt. If making flavored kale chips, add the other ingredients as well, in addition to the basic kale chips ingredients. Toss, using your hands to gently massage the kale to make sure each leaf is well coated.
4. Preheat air fryer to 325 degrees F (163 degrees C).
5. Place kale in the air fryer basket. (You can cook in 2 batches if it doesn't all fit.) Cook for 3 minutes, then shake the basket and cook for another 2-3 minutes, until the air fryer kale chips are crispy and dried out.
6. For lemon garlic, chili lime, or salt and vinegar, or flamin' hot kale chips, add an extra 1-2 minutes. For BBQ kale chips, add an extra 3-4 minutes.

Printed in Great Britain
by Amazon